D1287160

Words

for Students of English

Words

for Students of English

VOLUME 8

A Vocabulary Series for ESL

Dawn E. McCormick

Lionel Menasche

Marilyn Smith Slaathaug

Judith L. Yogman

 PITT SERIES IN ENGLISH AS A SECOND LANGUAGE

Ann Arbor
The University of Michigan Press

Copyright © by the University of Michigan 2004
All rights reserved
ISBN 0-472-08948-X
Published in the United States of America by
The University of Michigan Press
Manufactured in the United States of America

2007   2006   2005   2004   4   3   2   1

No part of this publication may be reproduced, stored
in a retrieval system, or transmitted in any form or by
any means, electronic, mechanical, or otherwise,
without the written permission of the publisher.

Contents

Foreword

The objective of this series of vocabulary texts for the student of English as a foreign language is to facilitate the learning of 4,100 new words and the contexts in which they occur. Second language vocabulary learning in the 1990s and early twenty-first century has become a central component in language teaching. This development is due in part to advances in theoretical applied linguistics that have recognized the central role played by knowledge of words. Vocabulary learning can no longer simply be about learning word lists. As learners develop communicative competence in their second language, they need to know words' morphosyntactic properties, they have to become aware of how semantic and conceptual features differ cross-linguistically, and they must be sensitive to frequent collocations. Advances in vocabulary learning and teaching have also been facilitated by electronic databases that make searchable corpora available to assist textbook writers in their preparation of pedagogical materials. In this way, materials can have an empirical base in natural language use by native speakers.

With the present lack of comprehensive vocabulary texts suitable for both classroom use and home study, this series is intended to support teachers in preparing effective vocabulary lessons so that they can meet their students' urgent need for an increased lexicon. We present here a selection of base vocabulary items and some of their derived forms (i.e., the noun, verb, adverb, and adjective of the same stem) together with a series of exercises designed to help students remember the new words and use them in context.

This text has been used in an experimental edition in the English Language Institute, and modifications suggested by its use have been incorporated in the present version. We hope that you find this new volume useful, and we welcome feedback on how it can be improved or extended to other lexical fields.

Alan Juffs
Director, English Language Institute
University of Pittsburgh

Acknowledgments

Volumes 1–7

A series such as this depends greatly on the cooperation and hard work of numerous people:

Christina Bratt Paulston and Holly Deemer Rogerson originated the idea for the series.

Christina Bratt Paulston provided ongoing support for the series.

Mary Newton Bruder, Carol Jasnow, Christina Bratt Paulston, and Holly Deemer Rogerson developed the first version of the list of approximately 600 words assumed known.

Holly Deemer Rogerson developed the original pool of words from which the 150 topic word lists were chosen. She also organized the word lists and provided general management of the project, including authors' drafts, revisions, editing, illustrations, duplicating, testing, and typing.

Ideas for word lists, format, and exercise types were contributed by Betsy Davis, Gary Esarey, Suzanne T. Hershelman, Carol Jasnow, Carol Moltz, Lionel Menasche, Holly Deemer Rogerson, Dorolyn Smith, and Linda M. Schmandt.

Final revisions of content were done by Lionel Menasche and Holly Deemer Rogerson, with input from classroom testing by Isabel Dillener, Caroline Haessly, Pat Furey, Carol Jasnow, Linda M. Schmandt, Jill Sherman, and Tom Swinscoe.

JoEllen Walker typed several drafts of the manuscript.

Lisa Krizmanich assisted during the testing phase.

Volume 8

Thanks to the following for their valuable contributions to the development of Volume 8:

Overall support of the project, including release time for some of the authors: Alan Juffs, Chair, Department of Linguistics and Director, English Language Institute, University of Pittsburgh; *assistance in developing word lists:* Gail Britanik, Janine Carlock, Jaime

Harker, Carol Jasnow, David Jasnow, Madalyn Mcneff, Christine O'Neill, Juli Parrish, Dee Strouse, and Lois Wilson; *usage judgments and comments on various exercises:* Michael Fender, Carol Jasnow, Dawn McCormick, Stephanie Maietta-Pircio, Greg Mizera, Christine O'Neill, Virginia Robson, Eric Slaathaug, Dorolyn Smith, Lois Wilson, Larry Yogman, and Mark Yogman; *classroom testing by teachers:* David Jelliffe, Dawn McCormick, and Lionel Menasche; *self-study pilot-testing of units:* students in the ESL classes ELI 5 and Linguistics 10 and the special "volunteer vocabulary class" at the University of Pittsburgh; *the idea of adding an eighth volume to the series and constant, insightful support:* Kelly Sippell, University of Michigan Press.

Introduction

Volume 8 of *Words for Students of English* takes the presentation of English vocabulary beyond the 3,700 words introduced in the first seven volumes. It introduces an additional 400 new words at the advanced level with collocations involving these words. The goal of Volume 8 is to teach generally useful words that are also of particular use to college students. The book is adaptable to many language teaching situations: it may be used as a core text for vocabulary learning classes or as a supplementary text in classes focusing on different skill areas. It can also be used for individual self-study.

While Volume 8 has a general format similar to the earlier volumes, there are some significant differences because it includes

- a strong focus on collocations, with a separate section for them in each unit
- modular units, allowing them to be taught in any order
- a companion Web site featuring two additional units (Economics and Law) and topic-related quotations for discussion.

Like the earlier volumes, Volume 8 includes the following features that have proved attractive to teachers using the textbooks:

- topic-related units that provide context for the new words
- in many units, inclusion of useful words that are not topic related
- availability of audiocassette recordings of the word form charts to provide an opportunity to listen to the pronunciation and repeat the words
- a word list at the end of the book for all the new words, indicating the unit in which they are introduced and including variant forms that cannot be easily derived from the listed form (e.g., *biodiversity* from *diversity*)
- sequencing of exercises within units from relatively easy and controlled to more difficult and communicative.

Selection of Words and Topics

In each of its 14 units, about 25 base words are presented. (*Base* refers to any form from which other forms are derived, e.g., *prestigious* derived from *prestige*.) The 400 new words and their collocations were chosen by the authors—experienced ESL instructors—

according to their usefulness for the intended audience of advanced, academically oriented learners. These words were then compared with those in volumes 1–7, and duplicates were omitted except in cases where the words are used in a different sense or context. The lists of a corpus were used as an additional guide for selection of words and collocations. The authors also conducted a survey of eight experienced ESL and non-ESL teachers familiar with the target audience to further refine the list.

The unit topics were chosen according to their communicative usefulness. While the topics have been selected to reflect areas of study frequently encountered in college, only general, less-specialized words that should be understood by any advanced learner were chosen for inclusion.

Collocations

Learning collocations depends to a large extent on learners' exposure to them in naturalistic contexts, but there is also growing interest in teaching them in the classroom as a significant element of language. According to Michael Lewis, "noticing collocations is a central pedagogical activity" (*Implementing the Lexical Approach,* 1997, 70). An example collocation is "news media" in Unit 1 of this volume; it is common, accurate, and idiomatic (unlike, say, "news givers" or "information media"). From classroom testing of the units it is clear that the concept of collocation is easy for students to understand. Thus, in addition to its 400 new words, Volume 8 indirectly introduces additional words by presenting common collocations involving the new words. These additional words may be explained by the teacher if the book is used in a classroom setting, or the students can look them up in their dictionaries. When selecting collocations, the authors made use of a database and also relied on their own knowledge of the language.

Format

The sections of each unit are
—Word Form Chart
—Definitions and Examples
—Exercises
—Collocations
—Exercises
—Discussion or Writing

- The **word form chart** presents the words categorized by part of speech.

- The next section, **definitions and examples**, gives the meanings of the words. Grammatical information is given in the definitions by means of the following conventions: "to" is used before a verb to indicate the verb form, articles are used with nouns whenever possible to indicate that the word is a noun, and parentheses enclose prepositions that may follow a verb.

This section, together with the word form chart, can be efficiently handled as work assigned for intensive individual study, followed by discussion in class of questions raised by students. At this point, the instructor may also wish to elaborate on certain definitions and give further examples.

- The first set of **exercises** is sequenced to take the student from easier, more controlled exercises through more difficult, less controlled ones, to a final phase with more communicative exercises. Exercise types vary among units, although there is enough consistency to make each unit feel familiar.

- Each **collocations** section provides a **list** of common collocations for the words in the unit, as well as a second set of **exercises** to engage students in noticing the collocations and thus to increase their familiarity with them.

- The **discussion or writing** sections include open-ended questions like those in the earlier volumes to promote speaking and/or writing practice. They may be handled orally in class, or instructors may request written responses. Also in accordance with principles of communicative language teaching, we have included on the companion Web site (http://www.press.umich.edu/esl/compsite/wordsforstudents), for each unit of this volume, a final exercise designed to elicit authentic, topic-related language use based on thought-provoking quotations as springboards for discussion. As in all highly communicative exercises, there is no guarantee that specific forms, grammatical or lexical, will be used. Nevertheless, it is essential to provide students with opportunities to be fully engaged in meaningful communication in which there is good potential for using their newly learned words and collocations. The instruction for this exercise therefore specifically tells students to work in pairs as they exchange opinions about the quotations. Instructors may then ask students to report their opinions to the whole class or write about the issues raised in one or more of the quotations.

The **Words in Volume 8** section of this book lists at least one form of each word in the word form charts. It includes the words in the two units, Economics and Law, that are on the Volume 8 Web site: http://www.press.umich.edu/esl/compsite/wordsforstudents

The **answer key** provides answers for all the exercises.

A Note for Students on Collocations

It is very useful to learn frequent collocations when you are learning new words. Therefore, in each unit we list some common collocations and provide exercises that focus on them. The word *collocation* refers to the way that words tend to occur more usually with, or near, certain other words. For example, *schedule* collocates with *daily* (*I don't like changes in my daily schedule*), *fork* occurs very often near *road* (*You'll come to a fork in the road*) and near *knife* (*Place a knife and fork on the table*). Sometimes words are referred to as collocating more or less strongly with each other. The strength of association between the words in a collocation varies greatly. Some collocations are almost fixed phrases, and others include words that are more loosely connected. The stronger or more frequent collocations are the ones emphasized in this book. In addition to studying the words and collocations in this book, try to make a habit of noticing collocations in all your reading and listening. This will help you to use your vocabulary in a more precise and natural way when you are speaking and writing.

Arts

Word Form Chart

NOUN	VERB	ADJECTIVE	ADVERB
acoustics		acoustic	acoustically
		contemporary	
continuum	continue	continuous	continuously
depiction	depict		
donation	donate	donated	
donor			
endorsement	endorse	endorsable	
exhibit	exhibit	exhibited	
exhibition			
exhibitor			
function	function	functional	functionally
		functioning	
fund	fund		
funding			
inevitability		inevitable	inevitably
installation	install		
lyrics		lyrical	lyrically
		lyric	
media			
medium			
obsession	obsess	obsessive	obsessively
origin	originate	original	originally
perception	perceive	perceptive	perceptively
		pristine	
semblance			
		seminal	
tribulation			
upheaval			
venue			
		vicarious	vicariously

Definitions and Examples

1. **(a) acoustics,** n. pl. {often used with *the*} [the qualities of a space that enable it to transmit sound]

   When they built the new performing arts center, the builders made sure that the acoustics were as close to perfect as possible.

   (b) acoustic, adj. [related to a musical instrument whose sound is not changed electronically]

   Many folk singers use acoustic instead of electric guitars when they perform.

2. **contemporary,** adj. [current; new; modern]

   The museum houses a wide collection of contemporary art, including very new pieces from this year.

   Contemporary writers are often compared to writers in the past, for example, *his writing style is similar to that of Ernest Hemingway.*

3. **continuum,** n. [a range that continues without stopping]

   Although we name the colors of the rainbow separately as *red, orange, yellow, green, blue, indigo, and violet,* the rainbow is actually a continuum of colors.

   For some individuals, "good" and "bad" are two distinct categories, but for others, "good" and "bad" are on opposite ends of a continuum.

4. **continuously,** adv. [without stopping or interruption]

   The orchestra played classical music continuously for three hours at the start of the festival.

   The college students played computer video games for twelve continuous hours.

5. **depict,** v. [to show or represent something in a drawing, painting, sculpture, or verbal description]

   The main character in the story is depicted as a fun-loving and foolish person.

   Ken's depiction of nature in his paintings is too abstract for me, but his use of color is interesting.

6. **donation,** n. [a contribution of money or goods to help a person or organization; a charitable gift]

> When blood supplies in a city are low, the Red Cross tries to increase blood donations by calling past donors and asking for their help.

> Many public art galleries and museums need donations of artwork and money in order to keep going.

7. **endorse,** v.t. [to support a person or an idea publicly]

> During the campaign for the presidency, both candidates endorsed education programs that focused on help for young artists.

> A product endorsement by a famous person can help increase sales of that product significantly.

8. **exhibition,** n. [a public show, especially one in which art or information is presented]

> The exhibition at the art museum explores how aluminum has been a part of our lives for 150 years.

> The coffee shop agreed to exhibit her photographs on their walls for one month.

9. **functional,** adj. [working; operating correctly; having a working purpose]

> Beautifully designed clothing and items for use in the home are sometimes called "functional art."

> The portable phone was not functioning because of the power outage.

10. **fund,** v.t. [to provide money for something]

> Her parents funded her college education, and she returned the favor by helping them financially when they retired.

> Funding for my favorite radio station comes from listeners, not the government or advertisers.

11. **inevitable,** adj. [cannot be avoided, certain]

> There is a saying that only two things are inevitable: death and taxes.

> The display of realistic photographs of terrible war scenes inevitably created a strong public reaction.

12. **installation,** n. [something put in a particular place for a particular function]

    In the art world, an installation refers to an art display intended for public viewing.

    We had to wait eight weeks to see the new exhibits in the museum because they first had to be installed.

13. **(a) lyrical,** adj. [expressing emotion and personal feeling, especially in an art form; having the quality of a song]

    Michael writes lyrical poetry about natural scenery and romantic love.

    (b) lyrics, n. pl. [the words of a song]

    I usually like the lyrics of folk songs because they express the feelings of ordinary people.

14. **media,** n. pl. {often used with *the*} [the various sources of information for the public, usually including radio, television, magazines, newspapers, and the Internet]

    Movie stars often complain that the media constantly try to find out about their private lives.

    When a business or government official wants to make an important announcement, a press conference is held so that media representatives can get the information.

15. **medium,** n. [a way of communicating; a type of material used for expressing feelings or ideas]

    Bronze was the sculptor's preferred medium for his statues.

    The common medium for reporting research results is a journal in which articles are reviewed by the researcher's peers.

16. **obsession,** n. [the condition of being extremely focused on or concerned about something, to an extent beyond what is usual or normal]

    Sebastian's obsession about perfecting his first musical composition annoyed his family and friends because it was all he would talk about.

    Kate was obsessed with her rock collection in her younger years, which may have been an indication that she would later become a geologist.

17. **originate,** v. i. [to start from a particular place or situation; to begin from a specific source]

> Many holiday traditions in the United States originated in other countries; for example, the jack-o'-lantern is from Ireland, and the Christmas tree is from Germany.

> He has lived in Brazil for twenty years, but he is originally from China.

18. **perceptive,** adj. [very skillful at noticing and observing]

> Artists are generally considered to be perceptive people who can understand what others are feeling or thinking even if they have not said a word.

> When we are tired, our perceptions are not as sharp as when we are well rested, so we are less likely to hear and see everything around us.

19. **pristine,** adj. [pure; undamaged]

> When I saw the used car, I was surprised that it was in such pristine condition.

> It took a lot of work to clean out the polluted river, but its water is now pristine.

20. **semblance,** n. [an outward appearance; a slight similarity to something]

> Although we do not have much time before the guests arrive, we should try to give the apartment some semblance of order.

> There is a semblance of peace in the country at this time, but the suppressed hostilities could easily turn into a civil war.

21. **seminal,** adj. [important for the future]

> Vincent van Gogh's originality had a seminal influence on later painters.

> All the students in the art history class are required to read the professor's seminal work on the subject.

22. **tribulation,** n. [suffering; trouble]

> After many trials and tribulations, she finally earned her degree in art history.

> For many artists, times of tribulation often come before periods of greater creativity.

23. **upheaval,** n. [a significant change, often violent]

> The verdict of the jury caused such an upheaval in the community that the police had to be called in to keep the peace.

> Being forced to take time off can cause emotional upheaval in individuals who are obsessed with working constantly.

24. **venue,** n. [the place of an event]

> The best venue for a summer concert is the amphitheater near the river.

> Due to the popularity of the pianist, the venue of her performance had to be changed to a larger hall.

25. **vicariously,** adv. [experiencing something through someone else when one cannot participate]

> Although Janet's parents lived far away, they experienced her college life vicariously because she kept them informed of all her activities.

> Since my friend's retirement from professional basketball, his participation in it has been vicarious: he attends basketball games as a spectator and watches them on TV.

Exercises

A. Match each word with its definition or synonym.

___ 1.	fund	a.	event place
___ 2.	pristine	b.	appearance
___ 3.	originate	c.	range
___ 4.	contemporary	d.	provide money
___ 5.	venue	e.	modern
___ 6.	donation	f.	nonelectronic
___ 7.	functional	g.	begin
___ 8.	semblance	h.	working
___ 9.	medium	i.	show
___ 10.	exhibit	j.	undamaged
___ 11.	acoustic	k.	material used for art
___ 12.	continuum	l.	expressing emotion
___ 13.	lyrical	m.	contribution or gift

B. Answer each question with a word from the word form chart. Use the correct form of the word in your answer.

1. If you were going to perform in a theater, what would you investigate to make sure that the audience would hear you well? _____

2. How would you describe a lake whose water is crystal clear? _____

3. How would you describe an event that you cannot stop or control? _____

4. If you give money to a charity, what do you call the gift? _____

5. What do you call a place where a performance is held? _____

6. If you wanted to publicize a big event, whom would you notify? _____

7. How would you describe a friend who knows you are sad even when you try to hide it? _____

8. How would you describe a piece of artwork that influences artists in the future? _____

9. What are you doing if you show or describe something in a work of art? _____

10. How do you refer to the words of a song? _____

C. Write *T* if the sentence is true and *F* if it is false.

____ 1. If someone displays only a semblance of intelligence, it is a sign that the individual is actually a genius.

____ 2. Contemporary music includes music written between 1800 and 1899.

____ 3. Installing a new front door on a house will require removing the old front door first.

____ 4. Funding their children's college education can be a serious concern for parents.

____ 5. If obsessed with a piece of music, a pianist may practice the piece of music day and night until he can play it perfectly.

___ 6. A continuum represents two clear choices.

___ 7. While traveling, one can send postcards and letters home to a friend to let her experience the trip vicariously.

___ 8. Serious illness and a death in the family are examples of tribulations one may experience in a lifetime.

___ 9. Inviting private guests to view a new piece of art in one's home is an example of an exhibition.

___ 10. A lyrical work of art is one that does not reflect personal feelings.

D. For each item, circle the word that is least related in meaning to the others.

1. pure	vicarious	pristine	clean
2. semblance	likeness	truth	appearance
3. previously	recently	formerly	originally
4. upheaval	calm	stability	rest
5. pay for	fund	finance	sell
6. support	endorse	approve	disapprove
7. pleasure	trial	ordeal	tribulation
8. receive	take in	donate	accept
9. contemporary	current	modern	antique
10. trivial	seminal	influential	significant

E. Complete each analogy with a word from the word form chart.

1. exhibition : gallery :: concert : _____

2. supposed : assumed :: appearance : _____

3. _____ : ending :: birth : death

4. donor : donation :: _____ : exhibition

5. heart : beating :: machine : _____

6. _____ : folk music :: electric : rock music

7. support : friend :: _____ : candidate

8. _____ : uninterested :: kind : cruel

F. Each of the following parts of a sentence includes a word from the word form chart. Complete each sentence in any logical way.

1. In order to help her deal with the tribulations in her life, she . . .

_____

2. One way to keep nature pristine is to . . .

_____

3. If a business owner wants to fund an expansion of the business but does not have money, she or he could . . .

_____

4. The media have a responsibility to . . .

_____

5. A tradition that originated in my community is . . .

_____

6. One thing that I believe is inevitable is . . .

_____

7. A continuous problem in the world today is . . .

_____

8. A realistic depiction of a situation is . . .

_____

9. An exciting adventure that I have experienced vicariously through a book or movie is . . .

_____

Collocations

1. **acoustic**—acoustic music; acoustic guitar; acoustic instrument; acoustic player

2. **contemporary**—contemporary style; contemporary design; contemporary look; contemporary art/music/dance

3. **continuum**—the space-time continuum; form a continuum; along a continuum; continuum from X to Y

4. **continuously**—continuous employment; continuous use; continuous process; almost continuously

5. **depiction**—clear depiction; graphic depiction; accurate depiction

6. **donation**—make a donation; generous donation; small donation; charitable donation; anonymous donor; generous donor

7. **endorse**—expect to endorse; refuse to endorse; give one's endorsement; withdraw one's endorsement; product endorsement; endorse a candidate

8. **exhibition**—art exhibition; have an exhibition; hold an exhibition; attend an exhibition; international exhibition; be on exhibit; exhibition hall

9. **functional**—fully functional; function properly; main function

10. **fund**—establish a fund; set up a fund; federally funded; approve funding; withdraw funding; emergency fund; trust fund

11. **inevitable**—inevitable comparisons; inevitable consequence; inevitable result; quite inevitable

12. **installation**—installation process; new installation; easy to install; permanently installed

13. **(a) lyrical**—lyrical style; lyrical music; lyrical poetry; lyrical images; lyrical portrayal

    (b) lyrics—write lyrics; compose lyrics

14. **media**—the media; mass media; news media; media coverage; media attention

15. **medium**—artistic medium; medium of instruction; medium of communication; medium of exchange

16. **obsess**—obsess over; obsess about; obsessed with; become obsessed with; obsessed with money; strong obsession; obsessive behavior

17. **originate**—originate from; originate an idea; have an origin in; of humble origin; of unknown origin

18. **perceptive**—depth perception; clear perception; very perceptive of someone

19. **pristine**—in pristine condition; pristine beaches; pristine area; pristine forest

20. **semblance**—some semblance of order; semblance of normality; any semblance of

21. **seminal**—seminal work; seminal essay; seminal study

22. **tribulation**—trials and tribulations; endure a tribulation; bear a tribulation; many tribulations

23. **upheaval**—major upheaval; violent upheaval; political upheaval; social upheaval; emotional upheaval

24. **venue**—change of venue; venue for; concert venue; event venue

25. **vicariously**—live vicariously through; vicariously experience; vicarious thrill

Exercises

G. **Circle the word or phrase that frequently collocates with the word in boldface. The first one is an example.**

1. **venue**	(change of)	replace	exchange
2. **seminal**	ticket	group	work
3. **exhibit**	be on	give	do over
4. **donor**	helpful	generous	instant
5. **installation**	theory	process	event
6. **fund**	settle a	exhibit a	establish a
7. **continuum**	by a	along a	around a
8. **vicariously**	dream	live	be
9. **origin**	close	dear	unknown
10. **function**	properly	ideally	closely
11. **endorsement**	purpose	product	problem
12. **perception**	height	width	depth
13. **lyrical**	poetry	textbook	editor

H. Complete the following sentences by using one of the collocations from the list below. Write the collocation in the blank. The first one is an example.

trials and tribulations	some semblance of order
in pristine condition	inevitable result
acoustic instruments	compose the lyrics
accurate depiction	major upheaval
contemporary look	along a continuum
approve funding	obsessed with money

1. Putting all the files into a cabinet gave the untidy office
   <u>some semblance of order</u> .

2. Moving from one country to another can be considered an example of a
   _____ in one's life.

3. Most self-help books are intended to help people cope with the
   _____ in their lives.

4. Although the old desk had been in my grandmother's attic for years, it was
   _____.

5. She was so _____ that she spent all her time
   working and therefore lost contact with her friends.

6. If the dean does not _____ additional
   _____ for next term, we will not be able to buy
   new reference materials.

7. The group sang beautifully, accompanying themselves on various
   _____.

8. I asked the person who cuts my hair to give me a more
   _____ because I was going to a special event.

9. An _____ of all the ice on the road was that
   some cars would skid out of control, and indeed an accident soon occurred.

10. I was expecting the painting to be unrealistic, but it was a(n)

    _____ of the scene and characters.

11. Sue does not think about most moral issues as if they are absolutely right or
    wrong; rather, her opinions fall somewhere _____.

12. I've developed the melody of the song, but I still have to

    _____.

Discussion or Writing

I. Answer the following questions.

1. What was the most memorable art exhibition that you have ever seen? Where
   was it? Why was it memorable?

2. What is a seminal contribution to art that someone has made in the last 100
   years?

3. Do you think good and bad art are clearly separate or two ends of a continuum?
   Explain your answer.

4. Do you think people should donate money to organizations that help the arts
   even though there are poor or homeless people in the community? Why or why
   not?

5. Do you know someone who experienced a great tribulation that he or she could
   not overcome? What was it? What was the consequence?

Business

Word Form Chart

NOUN	VERB	ADJECTIVE	ADVERB
allocation	allocate	allocatable allocated	
brainstorming	brainstorm		
client			
clientele			
credibility		credible	credibly
discount	discount	discount	
discretion		discreet	discreetly
entrepreneur		entrepreneurial	
entrepreneurship			
exploitation	exploit		
innovation	innovate	innovative	innovatively
innovator			
market	market	marketable	
marketability		marketing	
marketer			
merger	merge		
negotiation	negotiate	negotiable	
negotiator			
patent	patent	patentable	
potential		potential	potentially
recession			
retail	retail	retail	
retailer			
retention	retain	retentive	retentively
sector			
trade	trade		
trader			
trademark	trademark		
vendor	vend	vending	
wholesaler		wholesale	

Definitions and Examples

1. **allocate,** v.t. [to allot; to assign; to give in a systematic way]

   Sales representatives were allocated to different regions.

   The allocation of funds to develop the project was inadequate.

2. **brainstorm,** v.t. [to discuss freely in order to get new ideas]

   When starting to write an essay, it is very useful to brainstorm ideas.

   Brainstorming is often used to generate possible strategies when creating new marketing plans.

3. **client,** n. [a customer; someone who receives services from a professional]

   Treating clients with respect and courtesy is vital in business relationships.

   The clientele of this successful accounting firm consists mainly of midsize businesses.

4. **credible,** adj. [that can be believed]

   It sounds like a credible story.

   Their advertising has low credibility because their claims are exaggerated.

5. **discount,** n. [a reduction from the full cost of something]

   When a product sells too slowly it is often discounted, resulting in higher sales.

   A discount in the price of a few items is often used to attract customers to a store, in the hope that they will also purchase other items at the full price.

6. **discreet,** adj. [able to maintain privacy of information that should be kept private]

   Employers want employees in research and development departments to be discreet, in order to prevent competitors from learning about new product ideas.

   Angela has always shown discretion, so I think she is unlikely to tell other people about our secret plan.

7. **entrepreneur,** n. [someone who sets up business activities that involve risk of loss]

   Entrepreneurs are important in capitalist economies.

   The entrepreneurial lifestyle is too stressful for some people.

8. **(a) exploit,** v.t. [to make full use of something or someone]

   The oil company intends to exploit all the petroleum reserves in the West Seas.

   (b) exploit, v.t. [to take unfair advantage of someone or something]

   When a firm exploits its employees, they may then form a workers' union to defend their rights.

9. **innovative,** adj. [new; having the ability to start something new]

   Innovative companies are usually the most successful.

   Successful businesses not only innovate, but also get the new products to market efficiently and maintain market share.

10. **marketable,** adj. [that can probably be sold to numerous buyers]

    Our research and development team invented two new machines, but only one was marketable because its cost of manufacture was reasonably low.

    It is difficult to market new cars that are extremely different in design, but adding only a few innovative features will increase the marketability of a new model.

11. **merge,** v.t. [join together]

    When the largest corporations in a business sector merge, they can easily create a monopoly.

    A merger between companies in the same type of business can lead to increased efficiency.

12. **(a) negotiate,** v.t. [to talk to other people in order to come to an agreement]

    Merger negotiations between the companies ended before they could come to an agreement.

    (b) negotiate, v.t. [to transfer something in exchange for another thing of equal value]

    A check is a "negotiable instrument" because it represents money.

13. **patent,** n. [official permission from a government giving the right to own an invention or any special design]

   Some clever inventors have patents on several innovative products.

   The government did not grant me a patent on my new kind of automatic umbrella opener because it was not different enough from those already in existence.

14. **potential,** adj. [having the ability to develop or change in the future; possible]

   The potential side effects of the new medicine are few.

   Technology has great potential to improve the life of people if it is used properly.

15. **recession,** n. [a reduction in general business and economic activity]

   Some people say that there is a recession in an economy when business activity goes down for two quarters in succession, that is, for six months.

   Many investors stopped buying stocks due to the recession.

16. **retail,** adj. [related to selling directly to consumers]

   In my small town, retail stores are owned by families.

   There are many kinds of retail business, ranging from individually owned firms to international ones like McDonalds.

17. **retain,** v.t. [to keep]

   The merger failed because each company wanted to retain control of the marketing division.

   Customer retention is increased if a store has regular sales and rewards frequent shoppers with special discounts.

18. **sector,** n. [part of a whole]

   The sales manager divided the region into different sectors and assigned sales personnel to each one, so that the whole area was covered.

   There are various elements in any economy, the most important being the industrial, agricultural, and financial sectors.

19. **trade,** n. [exchange of one thing for another; exchange of money for goods or goods for goods]

   Free trade between two nations is often hard to achieve because each wants to protect its own businesses.

   Marketplaces have always existed because people want to trade products, goods, and services.

20. **trademark,** n. [a name or symbol legally belonging to one business or organization]

There are many kinds of trademark, such as names, designs, symbols, pictures, abbreviations, and special words.

Some trademarks become so widely known that they are valuable marketing tools for a company.

21. **vendor,** n. [seller]

Vending machines can be quite profitable if placed in high-traffic locations.

"Fast & Delicious, Inc." is a vendor of food services to schools and hospitals.

22. **wholesale,** adj. [related to selling in large amounts to businesses that deal directly with consumers]

Wholesale prices are normally available to retailers only and not to consumers.

Wholesalers buy goods from manufacturers to sell to retailers.

Exercises

A. Match each word with its definition or synonym.

___ 1. allocate	a.	join together
___ 2. brainstorm	b.	make use of
___ 3. client	c.	that can be sold
___ 4. credible	d.	discuss to reach an agreement
___ 5. discount	e.	discuss freely
___ 6. discreet	f.	person who starts a business
___ 7. entrepreneur	g.	official ownership of a design or invention
___ 8. exploit	h.	recipient of professional services
___ 9. marketable	i.	believable
___ 10. merge	j.	assign
___ 11. negotiate	k.	cost reduction
___ 12. patent	l.	able to maintain privacy

B. Answer each question with a word from the word form chart. Use the correct form of the word in your answer.

1. What type of businessperson buys large amounts from factories and sells to retailers? _____

2. What do you call a person who sells a product? _____

3. If something is able to develop, what does it have? _____

4. What do you call an economic situation in which business activity is generally reduced? _____

5. Who buys from a wholesaler in order to sell to consumers? _____

6. What is a part of something? _____

7. If you are keeping something, what are you doing? _____

8. What do you call a person who buys or sells in exchange for products or goods? _____

9. What is a company's official symbol or name called? _____

C. Write *T* if the sentence is true and *F* if it is false.

____ 1. Trademarks are grades received for selling well.

____ 2. Vendors sell products.

____ 3. An idea with potential is completely useless.

____ 4. Brainstorming is an attempt to get good ideas.

____ 5. Buyers are usually happy to get a discount.

____ 6. A discreet person will tell your secrets.

____ 7. Negotiation is meant to lead to compromise.

____ 8. Retailers sell goods to wholesalers.

____ 9. Inventors do not like owning patents.

____ 10. A sector sells products.

____ 11. Businesses like to retain customers.

___ 12. A small clientele is good for business.

___ 13. An employer who exploits workers is helping them.

D. For each item, circle the word or phrase that is least related in meaning to the others.

1.	retail	recession	vend
2.	entrepreneur	seller	merger
3.	reduce	innovate	discount
4.	principal	potential	possible
5.	recession	decrease	exploitation
6.	part	secret	sector
7.	trademark	trade	symbol
8.	client	wholesaler	retailer
9.	innovation	invention	invitation
10.	customer	vendor	client

E. Complete each analogy with a word from the word form chart.

1. doctor : patient :: vendor : _____

2. whole : _____ :: body : foot

3. _____ : new :: tradition : old

4. signature : person :: _____ : business

5. price increase : _____ :: addition : reduction

6. work : product :: _____ : idea

7. _____ : business :: writer : book

8. discuss : plan :: _____ : contract

F. Read the passage. Then, in each blank, write the most appropriate word from the choices in parentheses.

The (1) _____ (patent, discount, recession) was over. Trade in all (2) _____ (vendors, sectors, exploits) of the economy was booming, including both (3) _____ (wholesale, clients, innovation) and retail, and some businesses were eager to take advantage of the situation. For example, Sugarcane Candy Company wanted to increase its sales in this good economic climate, but its executives were not certain about how best to do so. They decided to call a meeting of all their salespersons and market analysts in order to do some (4) _____ (discretion, brainstorming, exploitation). The chief executive officer, Alvin Morris, invited the employees to be very free and imaginative in their suggestions.

Many ideas were presented for consideration. Magdalene Martin thought that more emphasis could be given to selling through (5) _____ (vending, trademark, merger) machines. Daniel Moore wanted the company to develop better public awareness of their (6) _____ (negotiation, allocation, trademark) through an increased presence on the Internet. Angus McTavish said they needed to (7) _____ (allocate, vend, market) many more salespersons to the northern sales (8) _____ (innovator, exploit, sector), where sales were not as high as in other areas. Telemarketing directed at small stores was suggested by Hyun Lee. Three sales representatives said Sugarcane should deeply (9) _____ (market, retail, discount) their products to wholesalers, who would then be able to offer lower prices to (10) _____ (retailers, traders, negotiators). Surprisingly, Vikki Gomez suggested that they should try to (11) _____ (retain, brainstorm, merge) with Sweetness, Inc., whose food products would complement those of Sugarcane, thus creating a larger company with better (12) _____ (entrepreneur, potential, discretion) to (13) _____ (vend, discount, exploit) current market conditions. The CEO, Morris, reminded her, however, that Sweetness was already (14) _____ (trading, innovating, negotiating) a possible merger with Ace Confectionery, Inc. Colleen Shaughnessy brought up the problem of (15) _____ (retaining, allocating, merging) the best salespersons because many of them were getting good, basic training from Sugarcane and then selling their expertise to other companies that were also aiming to increase their marketing capability. At the end, Morris told the meeting that Sugarcane had applied for a (16) _____ (sector, client, patent) on a new, long-lasting chewing gum, but it would not be available soon enough to help with the company's immediate sales needs.

The management took careful note of all the suggestions and thanked everyone present for helping to generate ideas. Before they left, the employees were asked to be (17) _____ (credible, discreet, entrepreneurial) about their discussions to prevent competitors learning about Sugarcane's new ideas.

Collocations

1. **allocate**—allocated to each; allocate resources; allocate fairly

2. **brainstorm**—brainstorm ideas; brainstorm plans; group brainstorming

3. **client**—private client; business client; professional client; serve a client; assist a client; help a client; regular clientele

4. **credible**—credible witness; gain or lose credibility; lack credibility; credibility gap; credible evidence; credible claim

5. **discount**—discount rate; percent discount; prepayment discount; discount voucher; discount coupon; discount store; offer a discount; negotiate a discount

6. **discreet**—absolute discretion; very discreet; discreet arrangement; exercise discretion; show discretion

7. **entrepreneur**—business entrepreneur; independent entrepreneur; successful entrepreneur; failed entrepreneur

8. **exploit**—exploit the potential; exploit resources; exploitation of resources; commercial exploitation

9. **innovate**—creativity and innovation; technological innovation; innovative ideas and concepts; recent innovation

10. **marketable**—marketable product; open market; stock market

11. **merge**—business merger; merge into; merge with; merger proposal; company merger; mergers and acquisitions

12. **negotiate**—negotiation process; peaceful negotiation; difficult negotiation; under negotiation; negotiated settlement; trade negotiation; labor negotiation

13. **patent**—apply for a patent; patent office; patent pending; patentable idea

14. **potential**—fulfill potential; realize potential; have potential; potential buyers and customers; potential benefit; potential market

15. **recession**—end of a recession; severe recession; recover from a recession

16. **retail**—retail sales; retail prices; retail market; retail merchant; retail outlet

17. **retain**—retain control; retain a position; retain power

18. **sector**—private sector; public sector; commercial sector

19. **trade**—trade agreement; international trade; trade practices; trade embargo; trade deficit; fair trade

20. **trademark**—registered trademark; corporate trademark; famous trademark

21. **vendor**—street vendor; licensed vendor; vending machine

22. **wholesale**—wholesale market; wholesale trade; wholesale merchant; wholesale outlet

Exercises

G. Circle two words in each list that frequently collocate with the word in boldface. The first one is an example.

1. **allocate**	exercises	(resources)	industry	(fairly)
2. **brainstorm**	rain	ideas	plans	increases
3. **client**	help	serve	produce	talk
4. **credible**	witness	patent	sector	evidence
5. **discount**	trademark	store	exploitation	rate
6. **discretion**	exercise	absolute	prevention	clientele
7. **entrepreneur**	successful	gateway	business	conservative
8. **exploitation**	resources	recession	retail	commercial
9. **innovative**	idea	concept	discretion	license
10. **market**	client	file	stock	open
11. **merger**	furniture	boom	proposal	with

12. **negotiation**	under	competitor	process	presentation
13. **patent**	pending	apply for	stand for	recession
14. **potential**	benefit	exercise	fulfill	credibility

H. **(a) Circle the word or phrase that frequently collocates with the word in boldface. Refer to the collocations list. The first one is an example.**

(b) Write a sentence using the collocation formed by the circled word or phrase and the word in boldface. Underline the collocation. The first one is an example.

1. **allocate**   knowledge   to each   maps

   The teacher <u>allocated</u> a book to each student.

2. **recession**   severe   trouble   range

   _____

3. **retail**   calendar   society   price

   _____

4. **retain**   probability   control   reaction

   _____

5. **sector**   private   approximate   color

   _____

6. **trade**   international   consumption   risk

   _____

7. **trademark**   essential   reasonable   famous

   _____

8. **vendor**   credible   licensed   solution

   _____

9. **wholesale**   merchant   patent   designer

   _____

Discussion or Writing

I. Answer the following questions.

1. What is the most popular type of store or market in your community?

2. What qualities make a person credible as a witness?

3. Describe a situation in which a person should behave discreetly.

4. Have you ever been involved in an important or difficult negotiation? What was it? What was your role in it? What was the outcome?

5. What causes a recession in a country's economy?

6. What innovations do you think will happen in the business world in the next ten years?

Communication

Word Form Chart

NOUN	VERB	ADJECTIVE	ADVERB
adaptation adaptability	adapt	adaptable	
amplification	amplify	amplified cellular	
confidentiality		confidential constructive	confidentially constructively
cynic cynicism		cynical	cynically
digression discrepancy	digress		
elaboration	elaborate	elaborate	elaborately
enlightenment feedback	enlighten	enlightened	
improvisation	improvise	improvised	
intention	intend	intentional	intentionally
interface	interface		
melodrama metaphor monologue		melodramatic metaphorical	melodramatically metaphorically
perception	perceive	perceptive	perceptively
pun	pun		
rhetoric		rhetorical	rhetorically
semantics		semantic	semantically
system	systematize	systematic	systematically
transmission	transmit		
understatement	understate verbalize	understated verbal	verbally

Definitions and Examples

→ adaptable, flexible

1. **adaptable,** adj. [flexible; able to adjust to new conditions easily]

   Some people are sometimes not as adaptable as others when it comes to accepting new technologies.

   When your business grows, you can adapt this phone system to take on different functions.

   → amplificación

2. **(a) amplification,** n. [explaining an idea more clearly and in greater detail]

   You need to amplify and develop the ideas in this section of your paper in order to make your point more clearly.

   (b) amplification, n. [the process of making a sound louder]

   Amplification of public speeches and musical performances through an electronic system is very common.

   → celular, teléfono

3. **cellular,** adj. [connected by transmitters for mobile radio-telephone communications]

   The cellular phone communication system's main problem is that it can be hard to get a good connection in certain areas.

   A good example of a revolution in telecommunications is the cellular telephone system.

   → confidencial

4. **confidentiality,** n. [privacy; the guarantee that what is spoken or written will not be revealed]

   Confidentiality is important to companies with a good reputation that want to sell products over the Internet.

   You cannot be sure that messages you send by email will remain confidential.

   → constructivo

5. **constructive,** adj. [useful; positive; practical]

   I always ask my roommate to give me constructive comments on my papers before I make my final changes.

   When one is making comments on someone's speech, it is not constructive to point out only what was wrong.

desconfiado / egoísta / pesimista

6. **cynical,** adj. [negative or pessimistic; showing little faith in human nature]

Peter has a cynical outlook on life; he thinks people all have selfish motives for their actions.

Jake's character on the TV show is a cynic, a bitter and negative man who is tired of life and wants to be left alone.

paréntesis / divagación

7. **digression,** n. [a departure from the main topic in speech or writing]

I hope the senator talks about his war experiences even though that would be a digression from his topic of environmental issues.

Politicians work very hard not to digress when they are speaking in public, so it is important for them to plan everything that they say very carefully.

discrepancia

8. **discrepancy,** n. [a difference in two versions of the same thing; an inconsistency]

If two people watch a crime take place, their stories will not be identical; there will always be discrepancies.

After Professor Thomas ran the experiment several more times, she began to see slight discrepancies in the results.

elaborar / desarrollar

9. **elaborate,** v.i., v.t. [to explain in more detail; to develop in more detail; to give more information]

Could you please elaborate on what you mean by a "metaphor"?

The vice president plans to elaborate his speech about health care to include references to all aspects of a national health insurance program.

iluminar

10. **enlighten,** v.t. [to inform someone about a subject]

In this lecture, I hope to enlighten you about the world of astrophysics.

I found that TV show on dinosaurs very enlightening and informative.

retroalimentación

11. **feedback,** n. [the information given to someone about his or her performance, test, or experiment results]

My job includes giving students feedback on their spoken English proficiency after I interview them.

Marketing specialists employ people to give them feedback on new advertisements so that they know what will help sell their products.

improvisar

12. **improvise,** v.t. [to do something in a hurry, with no planning; to act in an unplanned way]

> If you are not prepared with the answers to these questions, you will just have to improvise and do your best.

> Because jazz musicians often improvise, composing while they play, much of their music is not written down.

intencional

13. **intentional,** adj. [done on purpose; planned or deliberate]

> The misleading exam question was intentional since the professor wanted to see if you really understood the material or if you were easily confused.

> The candidate has been intentionally vague about her position on the energy crisis because she does not want to say anything that might turn voters against her.

interconexión / interrelación

14. **interface,** n. [the point where interaction occurs between two systems or two groups of people]

> Part of Alice's job in the public relations department is to act as interface between the mayor and the media.

> This program will help your computer interface with the software for the digital camera.

melodramático / emocional / exagerado

15. **melodramatic,** adj. [very emotional, exaggerated, or sensational]

> This broadcaster often uses a very melodramatic style when presenting news stories about natural disasters.

> The new play at the local theater is a melodrama about a young man who falls in love with an older woman.

metáfora

16. **metaphor,** n. [describing an object as if it were something completely different in order to make an effective and colorful comparison]

> You are using a metaphor if you say that the mother was a lioness defending her children against the bullies.

> Metaphorical expressions are a basic element of poetry.

monólogo

17. **monologue,** n. [a long speech by one person]

> In the middle of the play, the main character is all alone on stage while he gives a dramatic monologue.

> Instead of taking turns in a conversation, Jeff often starts a long monologue.

percepción

18. perception, n. [the realization or understanding of something]

Our perception of other cultures is strongly influenced by our own cultural background.

How an individual perceives a national tragedy depends to a large extent on how it is presented in the media.

juego de palabras

19. pun, n. [a joke made by playing with different meanings of a word or by playing with words that sound the same but have different meanings or spellings]

Puns in a foreign language are usually very hard to understand.

People rarely agree on whether or not a particular pun is funny; for example, "He *ate eight* cakes *for four* reasons, and it was *two (too) too* much" amuses some people but not others.

retórico

20. rhetorical, adj. [related to the effective use of patterns of speaking and writing designed to persuade or impress]

Students learning about writing often practice using different rhetorical or organizational patterns, such as comparison, chronological order, and classification.

The rhetoric of the preacher was characterized by scriptural quotations and much repetition of key words and phrases.

Pregunta retórica

21. rhetorical question, n. [a question that is asked only to have an effect on the listener or reader and that does not require an answer]

To get their listeners thinking, professors often ask rhetorical questions when giving a lecture.

When making speeches during an election campaign, politicians often ask their audiences rhetorical questions, such as "Do you want improved city services?" and "Do we want our children to be safe?"

semántico

22. semantics, n. [the study of meaning in language; the meaning of words]

Dr. Mortensen's lecture on semantics covers historical shifts in word meanings as well as current slang usage.

People sometimes say "That's just a matter of semantics" to express the idea that everything depends on how one personally interprets the meaning of a statement.

, sistemático

23. systematic, adj. [in an organized and regular manner; using a system]

The auto industry is doing a systematic study of new car buyers so that it can market its cars more effectively.

The accountant systematically reviewed the company's financial information for the past five years before making recommendations for the future.

, transmitir

24. transmit, v.t. [pass along; send; broadcast]

Our local radio station has a large new tower that transmits the radio signal to a wider area now.

We automatically transmit the data from this office over the phone lines every night to a backup computer in the government's central office.

, subestimación

25. understatement, n. [a description that represents something as less than it really is]

To say that the earthquakes in Mexico City caused some damage is a huge understatement.

The newspapers have greatly understated the need for relief supplies for survivors of the hurricane.

, verbal

26. verbal, adj. [having to do with spoken words; related to words in general]

A verbal agreement is as good as a written contract in some legal systems, but people generally prefer to have important agreements in writing.

A complete test of verbal ability evaluates all four skills: listening, speaking, reading, and writing.

Exercises

A. Match each word with its opposite.

_d_ 1. intentional	a.	prepare
_g_ 2. understatement	b.	destructive
_h_ 3. monologue	c.	emotionless
_i_ 4. cynical	d.	accidental
_b_ 5. constructive	e.	inflexible
_c_ 6. melodramatic	f.	public

_a_ 7. improvise   g. exaggeration

_j_ 8. systematic   h. dialogue

_f_ 9. confidential   i. hopeful

_e_ 10. adaptable   j. random

B. Replace the word or phrase in boldface with a word from the word form chart.

1. The radio station will **send out** the emergency signal on a test basis every three months. ___transmit___

2. This TV program concerning recent breakthroughs in AIDS research should **inform** the public of current developments in the field. ___enlighten___

3. On some interview programs, the host will let the guest **wander** in his answers and talk about anything he wants to. ___degress___

4. There is a **difference** in your accounts of the accident; one of you says it happened at 6:00 P.M. and the other says 8:00 P.M. ___discrepancy___

5. The listening audience has the general **opinion** that the newscasters are all well-dressed, highly educated, and intelligent people. ___perception___

6. Biochemistry is a science that developed at the **intersection** of biology and chemistry. ___interface___

7. When the police call, they will ask you to give a **spoken** description of the thief. ___verbal___

8. We could discuss this statement for hours because it's really just a question of **how we each understand the meaning of the words**. ___semantics___

9. The **speaking style** of some television commentators gets very boring after you have listened to them for a while. ___rethorical___

10. It is a **play on words** if you talk about electricians keeping current with developments in their field because the word *current* has two meanings: "up to date," and "a stream of electricity." ___pun___

C. Answer each question with a word from the word form chart. Use the correct form of the word in your answer.

1. What do you call making things larger and clearer? _____

2. How do you refer to wireless phones? ___cellular___

3. If a marketing survey asks you how well you like a new product, what information is the company looking for? ___feedback___

4. What word describes the comparison in the sentence "You are an angel"? ___metaphor___

5. If I want you to expand on an idea and tell me more about it, what do I want you to do? ___elaborat___

6. Which word refers to making something up without preparation? ___improvise___

7. What do you call a play on words using two words that are pronounced the same but spelled differently? ___pun___

8. What do you call it if I do something on purpose? ___intentional___

9. What word describes the point, surface, or place where there is communication between two different bodies? ___interface___

10. What is another word for private? ___confidential___

D. Write *T* if the sentence is True and *F* if it is False.

_F_ 1. Cellular phones were one of the first types of telephone communication invented.

_T_ 2. To amplify something is to understate its qualities.

_T_ 3. A monologue is spoken by only one person.

_T_ 4. If someone tells you something in confidence, she expects that you will keep it a secret.

_F_ 5. A cynical person is generally pleasant to be around.

_F_ 6. A metaphor can be purchased at any good bookstore.

_F_ 7. Semantics are a type of radio frequency.

_T_ 8. A species that is adaptable to changes in the environment will have a good chance of survival.

_F_ 9. A rhetorical question requires an answer.

E. In the space provided, write a word from the word form chart similar in meaning to each group of words.

1. private, secret, personal, _confidential_

2. emotional, colorful, sensational, _melodramatic_

3. impression, feeling, observation, _perception_

4. organized, methodical, efficient, _systematic_

5. accommodating, flexible, easygoing, _adaptable_

6. helpful, positive, encouraging, _constructive_

7. wander, ramble, deviate, _digression_

8. instruct, inform, explain, elaborate, _enlighten_

F. Complete each analogy with a word from the word form chart.

1. exaggerate : _____ :: inflate : deflate

2. _____ : confuse :: reveal : conceal

3. organized : planned :: _____ : spontaneous

4. depressed : _____ :: cheerful : optimistic

5. careless : organized :: random : _____

6. _____ : student :: opinion polls : politicians

7. fax : send :: signal : _____

8. musical : pianist :: _____ : speechwriter

9. _____ : joke :: jazz : music

10. drawing : picture :: comparison : _____

G. Read the passage. Then, in each blank, write the most appropriate word from the choices in parentheses.

Election year in the United States can be a very intense time. Candidates are constantly working to improve their ratings in the polls, giving speeches, and making appearances. To say that they get some help in preparing speeches is a(n) (1) _____ (understatement, discrepancy, monologue). Speeches are never (2) _____ (adaptive, improvised, confidential). Before the candidate ever appears publicly, he or she is coached in (3) _____ (confidential, cynical, cellular) sessions closed to outsiders, in which public speaking experts offer (4) _____ (intentional, melodramatic, constructive) criticism. These experts are trained to approach this task (5) _____ (systematically, adaptively, metaphorically), analyzing many different aspects of the candidate's speaking skills. They also study the text of the speech closely, to help the candidate develop an effective (6) _____ (semantic, rhetorical, pun) style. They make sure that there are no unintended (7) _____ (interfaces, feedback, puns) that may confuse or offend someone, and they consider the (8) _____ (interface, cynics, semantics) of the speech, to be sure that they cannot be misinterpreted.

A public speech is like a long (9) _____ (monologue, perception, understatement) in a theater play; the candidate is speaking on stage all alone for a length of time, and he needs to hold his listeners' attention and catch them up in his vision of the future. A/An (10) _____ (intentional, melodramatic, improvised) speaker will often be more successful than a boring one, no matter what his political beliefs are.

Speakers must be careful to stick to the topic and the prepared speech; if they (11) _____ (digress, interface, amplify) and talk about things they have not prepared, it can get them into a lot of trouble. They may accidentally insult someone or raise questions that they are not prepared to answer, making them look foolish. Many intelligent and hard-working candidates drop out as the campaign progresses because their (12) _____ (feedback, cynical, verbal) skills are not equal to the task.

The (13) _____ (adaptive, cynical, cellular) observer may

argue that campaign speeches are not worth listening to, that they are not meant to

(14) _____ (digress, improvise, enlighten) and inform the listeners

at all because the information and the images that are presented are so carefully

controlled. In addition, the cynics say that because candidates work so closely with

political advisers who give them constant (15) _____ (feedback,

rhetoric, understatements) on the public (16) _____ (interface, per-

ception, metaphor) of their campaign, there is very little that is spontaneous, and

politicians must therefore be considered merely as actors.

Collocations

1. **adaptable**—highly adaptable; readily adaptable; easily adaptable

2. **amplification**—speech amplification; amplification system; amplified guitar; amplify a sound

3. **cellular**—mobile cellular telephone; digital cellular network; cellular phone; cellular service; cellular pager

4. **confidentiality**—complete confidentiality; client confidentiality; breach of confidentiality; guarantee confidentiality; strict confidentiality; for reasons of confidentiality; ensure confidentiality; private and confidential; confidential information

5. **constructive**—constructive criticism; constructive dialogue; useful and constructive; constructive purposes; in a constructive manner; positive and constructive

6. **cynical**—cynical attitude; openly cynical; becoming cynical about; cynical comment

7. **digression**—needless digression; slight digression; long digression; digression from; brief digression

8. **discrepancy**—apparent discrepancy; discrepancy between; major discrepancy; wide discrepancy; reveal a discrepancy; little discrepancy

9. **elaboration**—further elaboration; elaboration and development; lengthy elaboration

10. **enlighten**—entertain and enlighten; educate and enlighten; strive to enlighten; enlightening account; make an effort to enlighten

11. **feedback**—visual feedback; get feedback; give feedback; constructive feedback; feedback systems; feedback mechanism; feedback loop; feedback session

12. **improvise**—ability to improvise; have to improvise; improvise as best you can; manage to improvise

13. **intentional**—purely intentional; not intentional; intentional action; intentional act

14. **interface**—explore the interface; user interface; interface with

15. **melodramatic**—melodramatic plot twists; melodramatic performance; ridiculously melodramatic

16. **metaphor**—it is a metaphor for (something); perfect metaphor for (something); functions as a metaphor; metaphorically speaking

17. **monologue**—final monologue; lengthy monologue; weighty monologue; spoken monologue; in the form of a monologue; angry monologue; uninterrupted monologue; dramatic monologue; internal monologue; deliver a monologue; brief monologue

18. **perception**—time perception; depth perception; extrasensory perception; reinforce the perception; public perception; popular perception; perceptive analysis

19. **pun**—obvious pun; make a pun; pun intended; no pun intended; bad pun

20. **rhetoric**—fiery rhetoric; political rhetoric; nationalist rhetoric; racist rhetoric; rhetorical question; rhetorical pattern; rhetorical device

21. **semantics**—a question of semantics; a matter of semantics; playing on semantics; mere semantics; semantic analysis

22. **systematic**—systematic approach; systematic changes; widespread and systematic; systematic study

23. **transmit**—transmit and receive; transmit a message; transmit clearly; transmit information; transmit a signal; transmit data; satellite transmission

24. **understatement**—something of an understatement; major understatement; huge understatement; the understatement of the year

25. **verbal**—verbal abuse; both verbal and physical; verbal battle; verbal skills; verbal confirmation; verbal contract

Exercises

H. (a) Circle the word or phrase that frequently collocates with the word in boldface. Refer to the collocations list. The first one is an example.

(b) Write a sentence using the collocation formed by the circled word or phrase and the word in boldface. Underline the collocation. The first one is an example.

1. **constructive**   thoughts   buildings   (criticism)

   Constructive criticism will help a person improve his performance

   and not make him feel bad about his weaknesses.

2. **improvise**   alone   as best you can   every morning

3. **pun**   obvious   thorough   quiet

4. **intentional**   sincerity   continuum   action

5. **enlighten**   educate   calculate   write down

6. **verbal**   attachments   decisions   skills

7. **monologue**   lengthy   bright   awful

_____

_____

8. **confidentiality**   cynical   strict   unusual

_____

_____

9. **cellular**   network   requirements   response

_____

_____

10. **melodramatic**   assignment   feature   performance

_____

_____

11. **transmit**   clearly   violently   happily

_____

_____

12. **elaboration**   further   colored   strong

_____

_____

I. **Complete the following sentences by using a collocation from the list below. Write the collocation in the blank. The first one is an example.**

fiery rhetoric	transmit data
question of semantics	brief digression
highly adaptable	get feedback
perfect metaphor	major discrepancy
openly cynical	systematic approach
reinforce the perception	something of an understatement

1. Good news reporters need <u>highly adaptable</u> personalities because they are always communicating with different kinds of people and moving from one environment to another.

2. There is a _____ between the number of people the radio reports as injured and the number that the TV reports.

3. Teachers can _____ on their use of teaching techniques simply by looking at test scores.

4. By carefully going through all their records, City Hall is using a _____ to identify and contact all citizens who have unpaid parking tickets.

5. Whoever thought of using the bull and the bear to describe the changing directions of a stock market came up with the _____.

6. Tobacco companies use advertisements showing beautiful women and handsome men smoking cigarettes in order to _____ that smoking is glamorous.

7. No matter how negative they feel, objective news reporters cannot be _____ about discouraging news.

8. If you will allow me a _____ from my main topic, I will tell you about my travels to Italy as a student.

9. The _____ of the young revolutionaries of the sixties scared many people of the older generation.

10. The new radio tower has the power to _____ to a much greater geographical area.

11. How you interpret the ambassador's remarks is really a _____.

12. Saying that the English spelling system is a little difficult is _____.

Discussion or Writing

J. Answer the following questions.

1. Should a reporter edit out inflammatory rhetoric when reporting on a world event? Give reasons for your answer.

2. How have cellular telephones and digital cameras changed the way we communicate with each other?

3. How can a company that sells products on the Internet keep its customer information confidential? Why would it want to?

4. How does the theater shape the public perception of major social issues?

5. Do you prefer to receive information about current events in a verbal or written form? Give reasons for your answer.

Computers

Word Form Chart

NOUN	VERB	ADJECTIVE	ADVERB
application			
backup	back up	backup	
browser	browse		
compatibility		compatible	compatibly
crash	crash		
cursor			
default		default	
download	download	downloading	
		downloaded	
encryption	encrypt	encrypted	
glitch			
hacker	hack		
hard copy			
hard drive			
home page			
icon			
installation	install	installing	
		installed	
	log on		
microchip			
network	network	networked	
output	output		
program	program		
programmer			
programming			
scroll	scroll	scrolling	
search engine			
software		software	
upgrade	upgrade	upgraded	
virus			

Definitions and Examples

1. **application,** n. [software that is not part of the computer system and that is designed for a specific function]

    On older computers, running more than two applications at the same time would cause problems.

    New computers come loaded with applications that let one write documents, gain access to the Internet, or process photos from a digital camera.

2. **back up,** v.t. [to make an extra copy of computer files in order to avoid losing them if there are technical problems]

    Many applications recommend that you back up your files every time you make any changes.

    Before I had a good backup system, I was always afraid of accidentally losing my work.

3. **browser,** n. [a computer program designed to give the user access to pages on the World Wide Web]

    Most personal computers sold today have a browser already installed.

    All browsers have a printer function that lets you print pages of a Web site.

4. **compatible,** adj. [able to coexist; able to be used in combination]

    Fortunately, the program I was using to manage my personal finances is compatible with my new computer's operating system.

    When buying a printer, you have to ensure that it is fully compatible with your computer in order to make full use of the computer's printing and graphics functions.

5. **crash,** v.i. [to come to a complete halt; to stop functioning]

    My computer crashed last night before I could get my paper printed out.

    Early computer models crashed often, causing the user to lose valuable time and work.

6. **cursor,** n. [a small movable line on the computer screen that flashes on and off and shows where the typing will appear]

> Make sure you have the cursor properly placed before you start typing.

> You can move the cursor two ways: with the mouse or with the keyboard arrows.

7. **default,** n. [the preselected option used by a computer program if the user has not chosen a specific alternative]

> If you do not change the margins when you type a paper, the word processing program will set them at the default.

> My sons like to turn the volume up on the computer, but I prefer the default setting, which is rather low.

8. **download,** v.t. [to transfer files from a distant computer or network to another computer]

> You can download many different games for children off the Internet for free.

> The download of some programs from the SoftComp Web site takes a long time.

9. **encrypt,** v.t. [to convert data to secret code so that unauthorized people cannot gain access to it]

> Most large Internet companies encrypt the data from a buyer's credit card to keep it secure from computer thieves.

> Data encryption is an important field of research.

10. **glitch,** n. [a fault with a computer program that suddenly and unpredictably causes problems or malfunctions]

> My email software suddenly developed a glitch that made it delete messages before I could read them.

> Software engineers run hundreds of tests on new programs in order to discover and eliminate any glitches.

11. **hacker,** n. [someone extremely skilled at working with computers; a computer expert who is very good at gaining unauthorized access to computer data]

> Most modern governments spend a lot of time and money keeping hackers out of official data banks.

> Some Hollywood movies make it look extremely easy for a skilled hacker to get anything he or she wants from a computer.

12. **hard copy,** n. [a printout on paper of a document on a computer]

> Mr. Shaw always makes hard copies of his most important email messages.

> I'll mail you a hard copy of this information next week, but for now I'm sending you the file as an attachment.

13. **hard drive,** n. [the magnetic disk inside a computer that reads, writes, and stores data]

> One important factor to consider in buying a computer is the capacity of the hard drive.

> We ran out of room for all our programs and games on our old hard drive.

14. **home page,** n. [the main page of any Web site]

> Most universities have a home page on the Internet that provides general information as well as links to sites with more specific information.

> My friends have designed a home page for their extended family, where they put up lots of photographs, especially of the children and grandchildren.

15. **icon,** n. [a symbol that appears on a computer monitor screen and represents one of several different applications or options the user can select]

> Most computer icons are designed to visually remind you of the program or the choice that they represent.

> Many people find it easier to choose from a list of icons rather than titles.

16. **install,** v.t. [to copy a program onto a hard drive so that it is ready for use]

> After you install this new Web browser, you will be able to work much more efficiently on the Internet.

> My computer crashed after I installed the software for my new printer.

17. **log on** {also **log in**}, v.i. [go through a set procedure to begin use of a computer system]

> Many Internet companies require you to choose a personal identification number to use when you want to log on.

> After logging in to a computer network, do not leave your computer unattended, because someone unauthorized might try to read your email messages.

18. **microchip,** n. [a tiny piece of silicon with a set of electronic parts, many of which are used inside a computer to make it work]

> With the invention of the microchip, computers went from being the size of several large rooms to being as small as a book.

> A computer's microchips could be called its "brain."

19. **network,** n. [a system of interconnected computers that can send data to each other; any group of items that are linked to each other in a way that resembles a net]

> All the branch offices of this bank communicate with each other effectively, because they are connected by a powerful computer network.

> Alan is a software specialist who helps companies network their computer systems more efficiently.

20. **output,** n. [a printout or results created by a computer program; the product of a process]

> Professor Simpson will reject any output that is not printed in standard form.

> This new software is able to analyze and output data at a very high speed.

21. **programmer,** n. [a person who is trained to write the coded instructions to control the operation of a computer]

> My neighbor is a computer programmer, and he usually helps us when we have trouble with our home computer.

> In order to enter the field of computer programming, you need a good background in math.

22. **scroll,** v.i. [to move the display on a computer screen, either vertically or horizontally]

> Scroll through the rest of the document until you get to the button labeled "continue."

> To move your document left and right, use the horizontal scroll bar at the bottom of the screen.

23. **search engine,** n. [a computer program that finds and organizes information about a particular topic on the Internet according to key terms that the user specifies]

> Some search engines are easier to use than others.

> You will get different results for the same key term from different search engines.

24. software, n. [programs or instructions to make a computer do specific tasks]

Harold wants to design computer software for video games.

There is a lot of entertaining and educational software available from Virtual Education, Inc.

25. upgrade, v.t. [to change to a more modern, improved version of something; to improve]

In order to improve its data processing speed, my company needs to upgrade all its computers.

You can often download an upgraded version of your operating system or other programs for free.

26. virus, n. [a computer program maliciously designed to be hidden and to damage another computer user's software]

The latest computer virus in the news arrived in a user's email with the subject given as *Family Pictures*.

Some computer viruses have been successful in causing damage to computers worldwide.

Exercises

A. Match each word or phrase with its definition or synonym.

____	1. hacker	a.	move information from one computer to another
____	2. network	b.	blinking vertical line on a monitor screen
____	3. output	c.	person who can get unauthorized access to data
____	4. download	d.	information produced by a computer program
____	5. hard copy	e.	able to be used together
____	6. cursor	f.	an interconnected system
____	7. compatible	g.	change into secret code
____	8. encrypt	h.	paper printout
____	9. programmer	i.	stop running
____	10. crash	j.	person who writes instructions for a computer

B. Write *T* if the sentence is true and *F* if it is false.

___ 1. An application is a type of calculator.

___ 2. A home page contains general information and is usually the first page you come to on a Web site.

___ 3. Every computer runs on a search engine.

___ 4. If two computers are compatible, they can share information easily.

___ 5. A glitch will make your computer run programs faster.

___ 6. You cannot use new software until you install it.

___ 7. To encrypt data is to translate it into a secret or private code.

___ 8. A computer virus can be easily seen by the computer user.

C. Circle the correct answers. Some questions will have more than one correct answer.

1. Which refer(s) to people?

   a. programmer   b. cursor   c. network   d. hacker

2. Which refer(s) to the Internet?

   a. microchip   b. home page   c. search engine   d. backup

3. Which refer(s) to an action you do on a computer?

   a. download   b. hard copy   c. log on   d. output

4. Which refer(s) to physical pieces of computer equipment?

   a. hard drive   b. software   c. upgrade   d. microchip

5. What do you want to avoid on your computer?

   a. log on   b. scroll   c. crash   d. virus

D. Substitute a word or phrase from the word form chart for the boldface words in these sentences.

1. Eric has a special external drive that he uses to **copy** his files onto every day, because he once lost a lot of valuable data when his hard drive crashed.
   _____

2. Inter-mart is a new company that is rapidly expanding and needs to know how to **connect** its computers in order to share files.
   _____

3. Molly wants to **get the improved version of** her software that lets her listen to music off the Internet. _____

4. The **small symbol** on the screen that represents items to be discarded looks like a garbage can. _____

5. The computer will go to an **automatic** setting for cursor speed unless you change it to your preference. _____

6. Some computers can launch the **software that enables you to hook up to the Internet** simply by pressing a button on the keyboard.
   _____

7. To **go through the procedures necessary to start using** this new software, please insert the first disk and follow the on-screen instructions.
   _____

8. When Will started playing his new computer game, the computer suddenly **stopped functioning.** _____

9. To enter your online banking account, click on the Web banking icon and **enter your name and password.** _____

10. My word processing program has developed a **sudden malfunction** that will not let me save my work. _____

E. **Read the following passage. Then, in each blank, write the most appropriate word or phrase from the word form chart. Use the correct form of the word or phrase. Some items may be used more than once. There may be more than one correct answer for a blank.**

When my parents began to learn to use a home computer about five years ago, they had a lot to learn. Unlike young people today, they hadn't been around computers all their lives, so even the most basic concepts and procedures were new to them. They immediately wanted to try out the different (1) _____ that came loaded on the computer to see what their purpose was and how to use them. My mother is a journalist, so she was especially interested in the word processing (2)_____. However, first they had to get comfortable with some of the beginning steps: how to move and click the mouse to get the (3)_____ where you want it on the screen, and how to (4)_____ through a document to move through it. Even the different (5)_____ on the screen, which represented the various programs, were at first a mystery to them. And of course, they had to learn how to change any (6)_____ settings to suit their preferences. Unfortunately, when they bought a program that couldn't run on their computer, they learned the hard way what it means for software to be (7)_____ with a computer model.

The first time their computer (8)_____, they panicked. The mouse wouldn't move, and nothing seemed to be working. They of course had no idea what to do. A neighbor was kind enough to come over and show them how to get it started again. However, my mom lost a lot of writing she had done because they didn't know anything about how to (9)_____ their work regularly. Now they have a very good (10)_____ system in place, and they copy any work they do onto floppy disks every day.

Once they became somewhat fluent on the computer, they decided to learn to use the Internet. They first attended a session at the public library that explained how to use key words in (11)_____ to find information on specific topics. They didn't have any software to access the Internet, so they had to purchase a (12)_____. Once it was (13)_____, and they chose an Internet service provider, they were ready to get going. Slowly but surely, they have been gaining confidence. My mom initially didn't want to buy anything over the Internet, as she was afraid to send her confidential credit card information over the computer lines. When we assured her that companies (14)_____ the data to keep thieves from gaining access to it, she agreed to give it a try.

Now they are much more confident. They even know how to (15)_____ useful applications from the Internet without any problems. They are in constant touch with their children and grandchildren via email. They are even thinking of designing their own (16)_____, which would include lots of information about the whole family. They don't panic when they encounter a (17)_____ that suddenly causes problems; they have some ideas on how to get going again. They are a little worried about being sent a computer (18)_____ that they don't recognize and that will destroy their files. But mostly they think using computers is fun. In fact, they have been enjoying it so much that they are ready to (19)_____ their computer system—they claim that they don't have enough room to run all the programs they want to and they need more (20)_____ space! I'm proud of them—they are staying young at heart by keeping up with the technology of the day.

F. Complete the crossword puzzle using words from the word form chart.

Across

1. You need to do this in case your computer crashes suddenly (two words).
5. A picture of a tiny printer on the monitor screen is an example of a(n) _____.
6. This causes unexpected problems.
8. When you transfer or move something onto your computer, you _____ it.
11. a person who knows how to write instructions for a computer
14. something you hope does not happen often to your computer
16. To do this is the first step in using new software.
18. the opposite of data that goes in
19. This blinks and can be moved all around the screen.
20. something you do to keep data secret and private
21. It comes from another computer and can make your computer lose information.

Down

1. To look at Web sites on the Internet you need a _____.
2. what you can do when your old computer does not do or store enough
3. a way to get computers to transmit information
4. a way to move around in a document
7. a general term for a program that does things like write text, compose music, or track your money
9. preselected setting
10. being able to work together
12. Hardware needs this to be able to operate.
13. the brains of a computer
15. computer expert who tries to access other users' computers
17. sign in (two words)

Collocations

1. **application**—computer application; network application; start an application; open an application; launch an application; quit an application

2. **backup**—backup computer; backup copy; backup disks; store and back up files; backup system; backup plan

3. **browser**—web browser; Internet browser; software browser

4. **compatible**—IBM compatible; fully compatible

5. **crash**—computer crash; program crash; network crash; system crash; disk crash

6. **cursor**—point the cursor; blinking cursor; position the cursor

7. **default**—default setting; change the default setting; default format; default printer; default font; default browser

8. **download**—free download; download a document; download an image; download data; download software files

9. **encrypt**—encrypt information; data encryption; encryption program; encryption software; encryption devices; encryption techniques

10. **glitch**—computer glitch; programming glitch; software glitch; technical glitch

11. **hacker**—computer hacker; anti-hacker software; network hacker; password hacker; attack by a hacker; defend against a hacker; secure against a hacker

12. **hard copy**—send a hard copy; print out a hard copy; keep a hard copy

13. **hard drive**—disk drive or hard drive; 100-megabyte hard drive; access the hard drive; install a new hard drive

14. **home page**—Internet home page; design a home page; set up a home page; develop a home page on the World Wide Web

15. **icon**—click on the icon; view as icons; desktop icon; file icon; hard drive icon; double click the icon

16. **install**—easy to install; install a computer program; install and operate; install software; install systems; uninstall

17. **log on**—log on to the Internet; log on to the server; log on to the network; log on to a site; log on to a remote computer

18. **microchip**—microchip processor; install a microchip; microchip technology; computer microchip; microchip revolution

19. **network**—access the network; local area network (LAN); computer network; network system; communications network

20. **output**—output and input; digital output; total output; output device; data output; printed output; program output

21. **programmer**—computer programmer; systems programmer

22. **scroll**—vertical scroll bar; horizontal scroll bar; scroll up; scroll down; scroll through a document; display a scroll bar; hide a scroll bar

23. **search engine**—powerful search engine; go to a search engine; use a search engine

24. **software**—computer software; install the software; software applications; software engineering; network software; interactive software; software programs; software specialist; file-sharing software; develop software

25. **upgrade**—service upgrade; simple upgrade; computer upgrade; upgrade a computer's operating system; upgrade the existing system; upgraded version

26. **virus**—computer virus; spread a virus; infected by a virus

Exercises

G. **Refer to the list of collocations to find one word or phrase that can combine with the following sets of words to form collocations. Write each collocation and circle the word or phrase that is common to each. The first one is an example.**

1. _____computer _____copy _____disks

   (backup) computer (backup) copy (backup) disks

2. _____ technology _____ revolution _____ processor

3. computer _____ programming _____ technical _____

4. local area _____ access the _____ computer _____

5. _____ setting _____ format _____ font

6. access the _____ install a new _____ 100-megabyte _____

7. _____ bar _____ up _____ down

8. _____ engineering _____ specialist _____ programs

9. Web _____ Internet _____ software _____

10. defend against a _____ attack by a _____
    secure against a _____

H. (a) **Match an adjective in column A with a noun in column B to form a collocation from the list of collocations. Some words may be used more than once. Write the collocations below. The first one is an example.**

A	B
blinking	upgrade
Internet	system
data	home page
backup	software
desktop	application
interactive	browser
simple	cursor
default	icon
computer	encryption
network	printer

Collocations

1. _computer application_   6. _____

2. _____   7. _____

3. _____   8. _____

4. _____   9. _____

5. _____   10. _____

(b) **Choose four of the collocations from (a) and write a sentence for each one. Underline each collocation. The first one is an example.**

Sentences

1. _I don't understand how to use the computer application for time management._

2. _____

_____

3. _____

_____

4. _____

_____

5. _____

_____

Discussion or Writing

I. Answer the following questions.

1. Do you think being a computer programmer would be an interesting occupation? Why or why not?

2. What kind of damage can a computer virus cause? What viruses have you heard about recently?

3. What can you expect to find on the home page of a large university's Web site?

4. Why is it important to be able to encrypt data sent over the Internet? Give as many reasons as you can.

5. What advantages are there to having your home computer on a network with your work computer?

Earth Science

Word Form Chart

NOUN	VERB	ADJECTIVE	ADVERB
		biodegradable	
carcinogen		carcinogenic	
detergent		detergent	
diversity	diversify	diverse	
biodiversity			
	endanger	endangered	
eruption	erupt	erupting	
extinction		extinct	
filter	filter	filterable	
food chain			
	give rise to		
habitat			
inhabitant	inhabit	inhabited	
herbicide			
lava			
monitor	monitor		
niche			
ozone			
ozone layer			
pesticide			
radiation	irradiate	irradiated	
reclamation	reclaim	reclaimed	
		reclaimable	
recycling	recycle	recycled	
smog		smoggy	
survival	survive	surviving	
survivor			
volcano		volcanic	volcanically
water table			

Definitions and Examples

1. **biodegradable,** adj. [able to be broken down into simpler forms by biological and chemical processes in the environment]

   Because too much detergent in rivers can kill fish and other organisms, environmentalists strongly advise using biodegradable detergents.

   Biodegradable herbicides and pesticides are unlikely to poison the environment.

2. **carcinogen,** n. [something that causes cancer]

   Asbestos, a substance that was once used to insulate buildings against fire, is a carcinogen.

   Some types of radiation, chemicals, and microorganisms are carcinogenic.

3. **detergent,** n. [a cleaning agent]

   Detergents often clean better than soap, but they can irritate the skin.

   Because the detergent most often used in the community was not biodegradable, the local rivers had suds in them.

4. **(a) diversity,** n. [difference; variety]

   Diverse organisms can inhabit the same environment.

   (b) biodiversity, n. [the variety of biological species]

   Many environmentalists consider biodiversity to be a good thing because organisms in a shared environment depend on each other in many ways.

5. **endanger,** v.t. [to put something or someone in danger]

   An endangered species is one which is in danger of becoming extinct because very few members of that species remain alive.

   A parent who allows a child to ride in a car without a seat belt endangers that child.

6. **erupt,** v.i. [to break out or break through suddenly; to push out hot liquids and gases from inside]

   The eruption of Mount St. Helens in 1980 blew the top off the mountain.

   Jennifer erupted angrily with accusations against her sister.

7. **extinction,** n. [the process by which the last individuals of a species die and the species as a whole dies out]

The dodo bird became extinct because it was tasty and easy to kill.

Scientists have proposed diverse explanations for the extinction of the dinosaurs.

8. **filter,** n. [a device for removing impurities from a gas or liquid]

Cities must find appropriate filters to purify wastewater that is a by-product of manufacturing processes.

Filtered water often tastes better than ordinary drinking water from the tap.

9. **food chain,** n. [the chain or ordered sequence of organisms that use each other as food sources]

A predator, such as a lion, is higher on the food chain than its prey.

The food chain for most environments includes microscopic life forms, plants, plant eaters, and meat eaters.

10. **give rise to,** v.t. [to cause or lead to]

Unregulated dumping of garbage can give rise to serious pollution problems.

Changes in the habitat gave rise to extinctions of species living in it.

11. **habitat,** n. [an organism's natural environment]

When a swamp is drained or a forest becomes farmland, a habitat is destroyed and a different one is created.

Many different species of plants and animals can coexist in the same habitat.

12. **herbicide,** n. [something that kills a plant]

Farmers are always looking for herbicides that will kill weeds but not harm crops.

A biodegradable herbicide will do its job and then break down in the environment.

13. **lava,** n. [hot liquid rock that comes from a volcano during an eruption]

During an eruption, lava can flow rapidly over hillsides and roads.

Steam and poisonous gases can escape from deep in the earth through lava tubes.

14. **monitor,** v.t. [to continually observe and record information about something's condition]

> Scientists monitor vibrations of the earth to predict eruptions and earthquakes.

> The hidden camera photographed the thief, and his image appeared on the security officer's monitor.

15. **niche,** n. [the role or place an organism occupies within its habitat, in relation to the other organisms that live there; a position that suits a person or a business within an organization or an environment]

> One niche within a habitat is that of top predator; this animal can eat many of the organisms below it on the food chain but is not eaten by the others.

> Rosemary did not do well in advertising but found her business niche in customer service.

16. **(a) ozone,** n. [a form of oxygen, common at high levels of the atmosphere]

> Ozone is sometimes used to purify water.

(b) ozone layer, n. [a high part of the atmosphere where ozone is concentrated]

> Some gases have been found to destroy ozone and make the ozone layer dangerously thin.

17. **pesticide,** n. [a substance for killing pests, usually insect pests]

> It is important to wash fruits and vegetables well to remove pesticides and herbicides.

> An insecticide is a specific type of pesticide.

18. **radiation,** n. [the process through which energy is emitted from a source; the energy that is emitted from a source]

> Heat, light, and X rays are all forms of radiation.

> The ozone layer filters out some possibly carcinogenic radiation from the sun.

19. **reclamation,** n. [the process of bringing waste land back to a usable condition; the process of deriving something useful from waste products]

> Reclamation of the bare hillside included planting grasses with strong roots that can hold the soil in place.

> To reclaim farmland that has been overused, farmers can plant certain crops that will enrich the soil.

20. **recycling,** n. [the process of collecting, processing or treating and then reusing discarded resources]

> We recycle our bottles, cans, and newspapers so that the paper, metal, and glass can be reused.

> Recycling scarce resources can reduce manufacturing costs and the amount of garbage that must be disposed of.

21. **smog,** n. [a form of air pollution; fog mixed with smoke]

> On a smoggy day, it is hard to see things in the distance, and the sky looks dirty.

> When smog is heavy, people with breathing difficulties should stay indoors.

22. **survival,** n. [the act of remaining alive; the state of continuing to live]

> "Survival of the fittest" means that the organisms that succeed in living and reproducing in an environment do so because they have some advantage over other organisms in that environment.

> Earthquake survivors often need help to rebuild their homes.

23. **volcano,** n. [a break in the surface of the earth from which lava, ash, and gases are sometimes pushed out abruptly and with great force; the mountain that forms around such an eruption, often having a depression or crater at the top]

> When we found out that the volcano was about to erupt, we decided not to visit Hawaii.

> Volcanic ash is very rich in minerals and good for the fertility of the soil.

24. **water table,** n. [the level of ground immediately on top of soil that is full of water]

> Where the water table is high, houses are built without basements to prevent water from leaking in.

> Builders must know the exact level of the water table before they can draw their plans.

Exercises

A. Match each word or phrase with its definition or synonym.

___ 1. diversity

___ 2. endanger

___ 3. extinction

___ 4. filter

___ 5. food chain

___ 6. give rise to

___ 7. herbicide

___ 8. monitor

___ 9. niche

___ 10. ozone

___ 11. recycling

___ 12. volcano

a. plant, animal, or business's special place

b. a kind of oxygen

c. using something again

d. a source of lava, gas, and ash

e. to keep on checking something's condition

f. a series of predators and prey

g. something to trap impurities

h. a plant-killer

i. variety of forms

j. the death of all members of a group

k. cause

l. to make unsafe

B. Answer each question with a word or phrase from the word form chart. Use the correct form of the word or phrase in your answer.

1. If we want to build a house with a basement, what has to be relatively low to prevent dampness? _____

2. What is something that can cause cancer? _____

3. If people bring water to the desert and grow crops there, what have they done?
_____

4. What can a volcano do that usually involves great force and melted rock?
_____

5. What is the term for a place where an animal or plant lives?
_____

6. What comes out of a volcano? _____

7. What do we call someone who is still alive after a disaster or a serious disease?

   _____

8. What might we use to kill insects that eat crops? _____

9. What is light a form of? _____

10. What can we use to wash our clothes? _____

11. On what kind of day can it be hard to see and breathe?

    _____

12. What is an important part of the atmosphere? _____

13. How do we describe a chemical that can be broken down into simpler parts easily or naturally? _____

C. Write *T* if the sentence is true and *F* if it is false.

____ 1. Lava that is flowing is hot.

____ 2. Biodegradable pesticides stay in the environment, unchanged, for a long time.

____ 3. A farmer may use herbicides so that the plants she is raising do not have to share food, water, and growing space with other, unwanted plants.

____ 4. Below the water table, the ground is dry.

____ 5. Human beings are extinct.

____ 6. Detergents help us to clean things.

____ 7. Radiation can be helpful or harmful.

____ 8. Smog is helpful to people who have difficulty breathing.

____ 9. People are lower on the food chain than chickens.

____ 10. If we have a lot of biodiversity in an environment, it will take a long time to list all of the plants and animals that live there.

____ 11. A species that fills an empty niche in an environment can probably survive there.

D. For each item, circle the word or phrase that is least related in meaning to the others.

1. water table	moisture	ozone
2. inhabitant	carcinogen	disease
3. diversity	uniqueness	variety
4. risk	endanger	monitor
5. explode	quiet	erupt
6. purify	filter	fill
7. give rise to	enlarge	produce
8. environment	survivor	habitat
9. ozone	oxygen	survival
10. review	recycling	reclamation
11. volcano	lava	reclamation

E. Complete each analogy with a word or phrase from the word form chart.

1. survival : _____ :: continuation : ending

2. smoke : _____ :: ingredient : mixture

3. pen : pencil :: _____ : soap

4. rock : _____ :: ice : water

5. filter : impurities :: _____ : radiation

6. _____ : cancer :: accident : injury

7. survival : death :: _____ : sameness

8. _____ : energy :: bird : animal

9. pot : cook :: _____ : purify

10. _____ : uniformity :: variety : sameness

11. hurt : help :: _____ : protect

12. _____ : ignore :: pay attention to : neglect

13. use again : discard :: _____ : throw away

F. Read the passage. Then, in each blank, write the most appropriate word or phrase from the choices in parentheses.

Most predictions about the world are not optimistic. Some environmental scientists and many other people expect the end of the world or the end of humanity to occur very soon. The only question seems to be what the cause will be. Will there be an accumulation of poisons in the environment, (1) _____ (monitoring, giving rise to, reclaiming) the (2) _____ (eruption, biodiversity, extinction) of life on Earth?

Most people are not worried by the statements of those who expect the (3) _____ (extinction, eruption, survival) of many (4) _____ (volcanoes, inhabitants, filters), serious floods, and earthquakes everywhere and all at once.

However, those predicting ecological disaster are most persuasive. They point to decreasing (5) _____ (reclamation, detergent, biodiversity) and suggest that when people destroy natural (6) _____ (pesticides, habitats, carcinogens) in order to build homes or factories, certain environmental (7) _____ (niches, ozone layers, reports) disappear. The animals or plants which occupy those (8) _____ (water tables, niches, volcanoes) then become (9) _____ (diverse, carcinogenic, endangered) or (10) _____ (extinct, filtered, inhabited). Animals higher on the (11) _____ (volcano, water table, food chain) which eat them may also die out. We are also reminded that nonbiodegradable herbicides, (12)_____ (inhabitants, lava, radiation, pesticides), and plastics can have very long-term, negative effects on people and other living things and their ability to (13) _____ (erupt, monitor, survive). Some extreme environmentalists even call for voluntary human extinction as the only way to reverse the negative impact of human beings on the planet!

However, nobody seems to talk about the recent reduction in amounts of pollution in developed countries. Can we predict that what a few countries have done so far, all countries can do eventually? If we work together, (14) _____ (monitoring, reclamation, water table) of badly used land, (15) _____ (eruption, lava, recycling) of resources and careful (16) _____ (diversity, endangering, monitoring) of the environment will help us to avoid or minimize many disasters and allow people to continue to live on this planet without destroying it.

G. Complete the crossword puzzle using words from the word form chart.

Across

1. can be broken down into smaller parts naturally
4. having all members of the group dead
6. to improve and put back in useful condition
7. with *to*, to cause (two words)
11. someone who still lives after a bad disease or accident
13. not safe
14. what takes something out of a mixture
17. something that can cause cancer
19. where things live
21. It's up high in the atmosphere. (2 words)
22. special places in a habitat or organization in which an organism or individual can do well
24. a cleaner

Down

2. use again
3. liquid rock
5. with -cide, something that kills unwanted creatures
8. to hit with a form of energy
9. with -cide, something that kills unwanted plants
10. a variety of life-forms
12. to push out with force
15. series of living things eating each other (two words)
16. to keep checking something to get information
18. with *water*, a level of the soil
20. what liquid rock comes from
23. a form of air pollution

Collocations

1. **biodegradable**—biodegradable substance; biodegradable pesticide; biodegradable chemical

2. **carcinogen**—potent carcinogen; weak carcinogen; potential carcinogen; dangerous carcinogen

3. **detergent**—biodegradable detergent; detergent residue; detergent action; household detergent

4. **(a) diversity**—ethnic diversity; religious diversity; racial diversity; diverse opinions

   (b) biodiversity—biodiversity treaty; issues of biodiversity; maintain biodiversity; sustain biodiversity; protect biodiversity; decrease biodiversity; destroy biodiversity

5. **endanger**—endangered species; endangering a child or minor; endanger the economy; endanger one's career

6. **erupt**—erupt into violence; volcanic eruption; erupting conflict

7. **extinct**—extinct species; mass extinction; become extinct; virtually extinct; extinction of the dinosaurs; extinct languages

8. **filter**—filtered water; filter out; filter through; coffee filter; oil filter; filter-tip cigarette; filtration systems

9. **food chain**—low on the food chain; high on the food chain; top of the food chain

10. **habitat**—natural habitat; principal habitat; wildlife habitat; loss of habitat; unique habitat; protected habitat; destruction of habitats

11. **herbicide**—biodegradable herbicide, herbicide-resistant; herbicide residue; herbicide persistence; herbicidal effect

12. **lava**—lava flow; molten lava; lava field

13. **monitor**—computer monitor; video monitor; monitor closely or carefully; monitor levels; monitor compliance; monitor a situation; heart monitor; monitoring devices

14. **niche**—environmental niche; find one's niche; carve out a niche; niche market; expanding niche; secure niche

15. **ozone**—ozone layer; ozone depletion; ozone hole; ozone level; ozone pollution

16. **ozone layer**—hole in the ozone layer; thinning of the ozone layer; threat to the ozone layer; protective ozone layer; saving the ozone layer; CFCs and the ozone layer

17. **pesticide**—pesticide residue; pesticide levels; biodegradable pesticide; pesticide-free; exposure to pesticides; application of pesticides

18. **radiation**—irradiated fruits and vegetables; radiation therapy; radiation warning; radiation dose; radiation poisoning; exposure to radiation; radiation levels; radiation leak; emit radiation; solar radiation; nuclear radiation; ultraviolet radiation

19. **reclamation**—environmental reclamation; reclamation projects; reclamation programs; reclaimed site; land reclamation

20. **recycling**—recycled paper; recycling bin; recycling program; recycling center; recycled water

21. **smog**—photochemical smog; urban smog; smog-prone areas; smog levels; smog alert

22. **survive**—survival of the fittest; surviving relative; struggle to survive; cancer survivor; barely survive; manage to survive; survive an ordeal; survive intact; survival rate; cannot survive much longer

23. **volcanic**—volcanic ash; volcanic island; volcanic activity; crater of a volcano; active volcano; extinct volcano; volcanic explosion

24. **water table**—high water table; low water table

Exercises

H. **Circle the words or phrases that can combine with the word in boldface to make a collocation. The first one is an example.**

1. **biodegradable**	food chain	(pesticide)	radiation
2. **habitat**	protected	ethnic	filtered
3. **biodiversity**	religious	treaty	ethnic
4. **diversity**	religious	active	ethnic
5. **reclamation**	plastic	glass	land
6. **water table**	filtered	high	diverse

7. **volcanic**	ash	seismology	carcinogen
8. **radiation**	furniture	warning	habitat
9. **herbicide**	endangered	biodegradable	reclaimed
10. **food chain**	high on	protected	irradiated
11. **filter**	coffee	water	lava

I. Replace the underlined parts of each sentence with a collocation from the collocations list. Part of the collocation has been provided in boldface. In the blank, write the rest of the collocation. The first one is an example.

1. There are many <u>people who are still alive after a serious, malignant disease</u> nowadays due to the great advances that have been made in medicine.

    Answer: **cancer** _____survivors_____

2. It is a good idea to wash fruits and vegetables to clean off <u>what is left of the chemicals that kill insects and that might harm someone who eats the food</u>.

    Answer: **pesticide** _____

3. It is important to add water to certain chemicals that have a strong <u>ability to clean</u>.

    Answer: _____ **action**

4. Dinosaurs are a(n) <u>large and diverse group of creatures that are not alive any more</u>.

    Answer: _____ **species**

5. In some countries there is <u>a situation in which people worship God in many different ways</u>.

    Answer: _____ **diversity**

6. I prefer to drink <u>a liquid that has had the impurities cleaned out</u> because I think it tastes better.

    Answer: _____ **water**

7. We read our email on a <u>device that looks like a TV</u>.

        Answer: **computer** _____

8. Scientists are afraid that reducing the<u> amount of special oxygen high in the atmosphere</u> will cause an increase in cases of skin cancer.

        Answer: **ozone** _____

9. A eucalyptus forest is a <u>one-of-a-kind place for certain organisms to live</u>, and koala bears will not survive in nature in any other place.

        Answer: **unique** _____

10. Sometimes <u>figuring out the perfect job and getting it</u> takes a few years.

        Answer: **finding one's** _____

11. A <u>land with water all around it, that has been formed from melted rock coming from under the earth,</u> can be a dangerous place to live.

        Answer: _____ **island**

12. The <u>special symbol telling people of the danger of certain kinds of energy</u> was painted on the door to the room.

        Answer: **radiation** _____

13. Strong sunlight may be only <u>something that will cause cancer not very often</u> for people with dark skins, but for light-skinned people it is more dangerous.

        Answer: **a weak** _____

14. (a) <u>A very small group of plants or animals that is becoming smaller</u> because the number of deaths is greater than the number of new individuals might be protected so that it does not (b) <u>die out</u>.

        (a) Answer: **an endangered** _____

        (b) Answer: **become** _____

15. We put our cans, bottles and newspapers into <u>special collection containers for materials that can be reused</u>.

     Answer: _____ **bins**

16. If you are interested in <u>improving the world we live in, to make badly used areas healthy and useful again</u>, you need to have a lot of scientific knowledge.

     Answer: **environmental** _____

Discussion or Writing

J. Answer the following questions.

1. Do human beings have the right to change the environment in order to make things convenient, safe, and pleasant for themselves if this means causing other species to become extinct? Why or why not?

2. What kinds of monitoring of the environment are likely to help people the most?

3. Do richer countries have a responsibility to help poorer countries control pollution? Why or why not?

4. How can biodiversity benefit human beings?

Education

Word Form Chart

NOUN	VERB	ADJECTIVE	ADVERB
accreditation	accredit	accredited	
acronym			
anachronism		anachronistic	anachronistically
anthology	anthologize		
collaboration	collaborate	collaborative	collaboratively
commencement			
curriculum		curricular	
dissertation			
elective	elect	elective	
facilitation	facilitate	facilitative	
framework			
humanities			
interim		interim	
ivory tower			
mainstreaming	mainstream		
margin		marginal	marginally
mentor	mentor		
minor	minor	minor	
pedagogy		pedagogical	pedagogically
plagiarism	plagiarize		
practicum			
profile	profile		
redundancy		redundant	
sabbatical			
syllabus			
transcript			

Definitions and Examples

1. **accredit,** v.t. [to evaluate an educational institution and certify that it meets professional standards]

   To apply to the university, you must have a diploma from an accredited high school.

   The university study abroad program is fully accredited; the classes you take in another country will count toward your degree in this country.

2. **acronym,** n. [a new word that is formed by using the first letter of each word of a phrase or name of an organization]

   NATO is the acronym for North Atlantic Treaty Organization.

   Most people do not realize that the words *scuba* (as in "scuba diving") and *radar* are acronyms formed from the phrases "**s**elf-**c**ontained **u**nderwater **b**reathing **a**pparatus" and "**ra**dio **d**etecting **a**nd **r**anging."

3. **anachronism,** n. [a custom or an event that is placed in the wrong time period; something that is old-fashioned]

   The modern hairstyles were an anachronism in the movie about cavemen.

   The professor's learning theories are anachronistic; almost no one holds such views any longer.

4. **anthology,** n. [a collection of paintings, songs, passages from literature or other works usually chosen because they are similar in some way]

   We are reading an anthology of short stories by female authors in our English literature course this semester.

   Our music professor is currently working on an anthology of protest songs from the sixties.

5. **collaborate,** v.i. [to work together on a project]

   The dean is interested in collaborating with other local universities on a study of why students drop out.

   The senior honors classes are a collaborative effort by the English and Sociology departments.

6. **commencement,** n. [a ceremony during which an educational institution awards degrees]

> I'm looking forward to commencement; I have worked hard for four years to get this degree.

> The graduating seniors get to choose a student speaker for the commencement ceremony.

7. **curriculum,** n. {plural: curricula} [the subjects in a course of study; a list of courses required for an educational program]

> The education curriculum is well designed; over four years, students cover all the current issues in education and get practical experience as well.

> Engineering students and psychology students follow different curricula starting with their first year.

8. **dissertation,** n. [a long and detailed research report written for a degree, usually a Ph.D.]

> Many Ph.D. students spend several years working on a dissertation.

> Sometimes the hardest part of writing a dissertation is selecting an appropriate topic.

9. **elective,** n. [a student's choice of class; a course that is not required for a specific degree program]

> My computer science friend loves art, so she completed her schedule with an elective in the art department.

> By their last two years of school most students have taken all their required courses, so they have the chance to take more electives.

10. **facilitate,** v.t. [to help make a process easier or quicker]

> The new online registration system should facilitate the registration process.

> Submitting your class papers via email will facilitate receiving comments and grades from the teacher.

11. **framework,** n. [a supporting structure, either for ideas or for concrete objects]

> In this course, we will give you a framework for understanding the main problems facing teachers today.

> This theory of early childhood learning does not fit into the traditional framework; it has some radical new ideas.

12. **humanities,** n. [the areas of study concerned with subjects like art, philosophy, literature, and history—as contrasted with areas involving sciences]

> Premedical students should take some courses in the humanities, like art appreciation and modern poetry, along with their science classes.

> Music is considered one of the humanities.

13. **interim,** n. [a period of time between two events; a condition or state that is temporary]

> The new dean of the business school is not able to start work until next semester; in the interim, the associate dean will be in charge.

> The university has appointed an interim dean of student affairs while it continues to take applications for the position.

14. **ivory tower,** n. [an imaginary place of knowledge and learning that is separate from the daily problems of real life]

> Professor Hyman is so lost in his ivory tower that he has very little idea of what his students are actually thinking and doing.

> Some people think that philosophy majors live in an ivory tower because their studies have no practical application in the real world.

15. **mainstreaming,** n. [the practice of placing students with special needs in schools for the general student population]

> Mainstreaming the special-needs student helps the rest of the student body to learn tolerance and understanding through having someone different in their classes.

> Years ago, most special-needs students were not mainstreamed at all; they were taught in separate classes and sometimes even separate schools.

16. **marginal,** adj. [being on the edge in some way; minimal; small; negligible]

> He was only marginally qualified for the job; he had some experience but not the right educational background.

> Homeless people are on the margins of society.

17. **mentor,** n. [a person with experience who will advise and help a less experienced person in work or career]

> If you have a good mentor in your department, he or she can help you plan your courses and use your time most effectively.

> Many successful professionals give credit for their achievements to the mentoring they received from senior colleagues who regularly gave them good advice.

18. **minor,** n. [a student's secondary course of study]

   A major in business and a minor in Spanish is a very useful combination.

   I need nine courses for my major in history and four for my minor in psychology.

19. **pedagogy,** n. [the art or science of education and teaching]

   A course in general pedagogy should include topics like student motivation and student learning styles.

   Pedagogical studies show that some children learn best in a noncompetitive setting.

20. **plagiarize,** n. [the act of copying someone else's work and claiming it as one's own]

   You are plagiarizing if you copy sentences from a textbook and use them in your own paper without quotation marks and citation of the source.

   There have been cases of famous novelists who have plagiarized the writing of others and have then said that it was done unconsciously.

21. **practicum,** n. [a course that offers actual experience in the field being studied]

   After three years of study in theory and methodology, education students usually do a supervised practicum for two months in a classroom.

   The practicum gives them the opportunity to put what they have learned into practice.

22. **profile,** n. [short biography; an outline of the main features of a character or group]

   We can study the psychological profiles of different learners to see what motivates them.

   Detectives try to profile certain types of criminals so that they can catch them before they strike again.

23. **redundancy,** n. [an unnecessary repetition of information; anything extra that is not needed]

   Many official publications are so full of redundancy that they are very tiresome to read.

   This paragraph of your paper is redundant; you have already stated this information in the introduction.

24. **sabbatical,** n. [a period of paid absence from work for a professor, during which she is expected to do research and work in her field]

   During my sabbatical, I will travel to the Galapagos Islands to do biological fieldwork on different species of tropical frogs.

   Most professors are eligible for a sabbatical only after seven years of teaching.

25. **syllabus,** n. {plural: syllabi, syllabuses} [the order of topics, assignments, and tests in a particular class; the overall plan for a class]

   The professor passed out the syllabus on the first day of class so we knew what the reading assignments would be for the whole semester.

   If you check your syllabus, you will see when the papers are due and how much they will count toward your final grade.

26. **transcript,** n. [a written, official record of a student's completed courses and grades from an educational institution]

   Most universities require a copy of your high school transcript as part of your application.

   The student records office charges a fee for making more than one copy of a student's transcript.

Exercises

A. Match each word with its definition or synonym.

_____ 1. practicum

_____ 2. curriculum

_____ 3. framework

_____ 4. profile

_____ 5. syllabus

_____ 6. anachronism

_____ 7. marginal

_____ 8. mentor

a. a more experienced person to help you in your career

b. repetition of information

c. including special needs students in regular classes

d. a temporary period of time

e. a period of practical work experience

f. a supporting structure

g. a word formed from the first letters of each word of the name of an organization

h. the subjects and courses in a program of study

_____ 9. interim   i.   information about someone's character

_____ 10. redundancy   j.   a list of the assignments and topics in a particular class

_____ 11. acronym   k.   something that is in the wrong time period

_____ 12. mainstreaming   l.   on the edge

B. Answer each question with a word or phrase from the word form chart. Use the correct form of the word or phrase in your answer.

1. What is the general term for the study of humans and their culture, for example, their religion, their artwork, and their literature?

   _____

2. If someone collects prints of all the paintings by a certain artist in one volume, what is such a volume called?_____

3. Taking someone else's ideas and writings and using them as if they are your own is doing what? _____

4. When professors work together on an experiment or writing a research paper, what are they doing? _____

5. What word refers to the study of how education and learning takes place?_____

6. What are the optional courses that a student may take after completing all required courses?_____

7. What is the term for the long and detailed research paper that a student writes to complete a Ph.D. degree? _____

8. What are you doing if you make something easier to do?

   _____

9. What is the term for the written record of all of a student's grades from a school? _____

10. What ceremony do you attend when you finish a college degree?

   _____

C. Write *T* if the sentence is true and *F* if it is false.

_____ 1. The ivory tower is a specific type of building that is found on most large campuses.

_____ 2. An accredited school assigns varying credits to classes depending on the amount of tuiton paid by each student.

_____ 3. A student has fewer requirements for a minor than for a major.

_____ 4. A sabbatical is a term for the long summer vacation that many professors take each year.

_____ 5. A dissertation is longer and more detailed than a class paper.

_____ 6. Your transcript will show all your grades, including any incomplete grades, and your grade point average.

_____ 7. Pedagogy is the study of how young children learn to read and write.

_____ 8. If you major in art history, you are a student in the humanities.

_____ 9. Commencement is a welcome ceremony at the beginning of your university studies.

_____ 10. For a piece of information to be redundant, it has to be repeated or be so obvious that it is clear without needing to be stated.

D. Circle the two words that are most similar in meaning.

1. mentor   guide   colleague

2. anthology   thesis   collection

3. plagiarize   copy   omit

4. important   marginal   minimal

5. profile   description   paragraph

6. redundant   brilliant   repetitive

7. guarantee   ease   facilitate

8. sabbatical   party   break

9. cooperate   collaborate   evaluate

10. judge   mainstream   include

E. Circle the correct answers. Some questions will have more than one correct answer.

1. Which refer(s) to work that people do together?

   a. elective   b. framework   c. collaboration   d. interim   e. pedagogy

2. Which refer(s) to a relationship between two people?

   a. marginal   b. profile   c. syllabus   d. anachronism   e. mentoring

3. What would most likely be followed by a party?

   a. mainstreaming   b. anthology   c. commencement
   d. framework   e. curriculum

4. Choose one word that can be used to describe a school.

   a. interim   b. practicum   c. syllabus   d. facilitated   e. accredited

5. Which can be written on a piece of paper?

   a. margin   b. syllabus   c. ivory tower   d. sabbatical   e. humanities

6. Which refer(s) to a period of time?

   a. acronym   b. elective   c. interim   d. sabbatical   e. plagiarism

F. Read the passage. Then, in each blank, write the most appropriate word or phrase from the word form chart. Use the correct form of the word or phrase. Some items may be used more than once.

The ceremony of (1) _____ is a very special time in students' lives, and there are many steps that lead up to this moment. Often it all begins in high school as the students study the published (2) _____ and curricula of various universities to learn more about them. Guidebooks to higher education list which universities and schools are fully (3) _____, which is very important in evaluating the worth of a college degree. They also help give students a (4) _____ for considering different places—by deciding what features are important in a university education, students can better decide where to apply. For example, do they want a school that offers them a chance to do a (5) _____ in their field so that they finish with actual work experience? Do they want to have access to sororities and fraternities (clubs for women and men) or do they feel these are out of date and (6) _____ in today's society? Do they want the opportunity to do graduate work and even to (7) _____ with professors in their field on research work? Or is it more important to find a (8) _____ in a small school who can help them get the most out of their undergraduate education and then help them plan for an advanced degree? Do they want a school which emphasizes the sciences and professional training for a specific occupation, or do they want one that is strong in the (9) _____, with professors who encourage their students to reflect on and learn about the world around them?

After they get information from the places they are interested in, they can examine the (10) _____ requirements for different majors. Then they fill out an application, send in the fee and a copy of their high school (11)_____, and wait for an answer.

Once they have been accepted and start their studies, the hard work really begins. After choosing a major, students follow a strict (12) _____ at first, taking all the required courses. Later they will have the opportunity to take some (13) _____, which might be things they really enjoy, such as modern dance or painting. For some, college is a time for self-exploration. For others, self-exploration is a (14) _____ concern, one that they are not very interested in; they are more focused on the practical career-oriented purpose of education. Some students take enough courses in a second field to (15) _____ in it. Many students come up with useful major and minor combinations that will (16) _____ their entering the working world, like business and Spanish or computer science and technical writing.

If they are receiving a Ph.D. degree, they are standing at the end of years of work. Writing a (17) _____ can take 2–4 years for some and even longer for others. It is well worth it, however, when the student hears her or his name called out to receive the diploma. Thus (18) _____ marks an end but also a beginning. It is the end of student days—it marks the time to leave the (19) _____ of college life and enter the working world. It is the beginning of a lifetime of learning through experience.

Collocations

1. **accredited**—fully accredited; approved and accredited; officially accredited; accredited through/by; receive accreditation; deny accreditation; accredited program

2. **acronym**—an acronym for; known by the acronym; acronym stands for

3. **anachronism**—become an anachronism; somewhat of an anachronism; complete anachronism

4. **anthology**—compile an anthology; publish an anthology

5. **collaboration**—a collaboration between/with; in collaboration with; collaborative effort

6. **commencement**—commencement address; commencement speech; commencement ceremony; commencement speaker; hold commencement exercises

7. **curriculum**—curriculum vitae; curriculum development; curriculum advisor; curriculum requirements; core curriculum; curricular emphasis

8. **dissertation**—Ph.D. dissertation; doctoral dissertation; dissertation topic; dissertation proposal; research dissertation; unpublished dissertation; write a dissertation; defend a dissertation

9. **elective**—elective courses; elective subjects; elective surgery; elective office

10. **facilitate**—facilitate an agreement; facilitate trade; facilitate business; facilitate communication; facilitate growth; facilitate development

11. **framework**—creating a framework for; provide a framework for; develop a framework; theoretical framework; useful framework; overall framework

12. **humanities**—a degree in the humanities; studies in the humanities; liberal arts and the humanities

13. **interim**—in the interim; interim leader; on an interim basis; serve on an interim basis; serve as interim manager; interim period

14. **ivory tower**—living in an ivory tower; isolated in an ivory tower; ivory tower intellectuals

15. **mainstreaming**—educational mainstreaming; mainstreaming special needs students; practice of mainstreaming

16. **marginal**—marginal effect; marginal areas; only marginally; wide margin; narrow margin

17. **mentor**—friend and mentor; become a mentor; be a mentor to; partner and mentor; a mentoring program

18. **minor**—minor ailments; minor injuries; relatively minor; minor in (a subject)

19. **pedagogy**—pedagogical theory; pedagogy of a subject; pedagogy course; pedagogical basis

20. **plagiarism**—full of plagiarism; plagiarize someone's writing; plagiarize from; guilty of plagiarism

21. **practicum**—student practicum; practicum site; practicum supervisor

22. **profile**—keep a low profile; high profile; raise a profile

23. **redundancy**—redundant words; make redundant

24. **sabbatical**—on sabbatical; a year's sabbatical; take a sabbatical from; brief sabbatical; sabbatical leave

25. **syllabus**—course syllabus; syllabus requirements; syllabus design

26. **transcript**—school transcript; copy of your transcript; listed on your transcript; formal transcript; official transcript; written transcript; full/partial transcript

Exercises

G. **In each sentence, circle the words or phrases that frequently collocate with the word in boldface. The first one is an example.**

1. Some manual workers were (made) **redundant** when automation was increased in the factory.

2. Let me introduce you to a wonderful person who is both my partner and my **mentor**.

3. The ideas you will study in this introductory course will provide you with a useful **framework** for advanced study.

4. The computer science department will be offering a new degree in **collaboration** with the department of philosophy.

5. While the administration conducts a search for a new dean of the school of law, Professor Jones has been appointed to serve on an **interim** basis.

6. Please be sure to include an official copy of your secondary school **transcript** with your application.

7. After five years of teaching, I am taking a **sabbatical**, starting next August.

8. The **curricular** emphasis of this nursing program is on preventive medicine.

9. The practice of **mainstreaming** is relatively new in public education.

10. The **commencement** address was so long and boring that most of the students fell asleep before it was over.

11. It is easy for the inexperienced writer to **plagiarize** unintentionally from sources when writing a research paper.

12. A degree in the **humanities** will prepare you to live your life to the fullest.

H. Select the appropriate word or phrase to complete the sentence. Refer to the collocations list. Choose the one that frequently collocates with the word in boldface. The first one is an example.

1. With her old fashioned hairstyle and manner of dressing, she is in danger of __becoming__ an **anachronism**.

   a. thinking like   b. seeing   c. becoming   d. throwing

2. Intellectuals who spend all their time studying things that have no practical value are accused of _____ an **ivory tower**.

   a. driving in   b. living in   c. grading in   d. correcting in

3. Students who are very active in student government and are often quoted in the campus newspaper have a _____ **profile**.

   a. high   b. well-defined   c. valuable   d. correct

4. There is a wealth of valuable research information in _____ **dissertations**.

   a. newspaper   b. secondary   c. unpublished   d. communicated

5. In order to find out what the assignments are for this course, look at the course description that the professor gave you; it has all the **syllabus**

   _____.

   a. listings   b. columns   c. pages   d. requirements

6. By collecting students' email addresses right away, we hope to **facilitate**
_____ between professor and students in this
course.

    a. writing   b. communication   c. grading   d. consultation

7. I plan to major in political science and **minor**
_____.

    a. after graduation   b. in economics   c. in the department   d. next year

8. One of the requirements for graduation is a(n)
_____ **practicum**.

    a. elective   b. complete   c. lengthy   d. student

I. Select the appropriate word or phrase to complete the sentence. Refer to the collocations list. Choose the one that frequently collocates with the word in boldface. The first one is an example.

1. When the new student orientation policy was implemented, it had only a
marginal _effect_ .

    a. effect   b. idea

2. I have to wait a year before I can take any **elective** _____.

    a. papers   b. courses

3. We are working to _____ an **anthology** of live performances by
early jazz musicians.

    a. manufacture   b. publish

4. The practice of teaching music in the public schools has a very sound
pedagogical _____.

    a. basis   b. habit

5. The Test of English as a Foreign Language is _____ the **acronym** TOEFL.

    a. carried into   b. known by

6. This new university program has not yet been _____ **accredited.**

    a. officially   b. hopefully

7. This book describes a(n) _____ **framework** that will help you to understand your experimental results.

    a. theoretical   b. anachronistic

8. Delete the **redundant** _____ in your introductory sentence.

    a. students   b. words

Discussion or Writing

J. Answer the following questions.

1. Is mainstreaming a common practice in your community? What is your opinion of this practice?

2. What university curriculum will best prepare future teachers?

3. Should college students majoring in a technical field be required to take certain courses in the humanities? Why or why not?

4. How can finding a mentor facilitate the academic career of a college student?

Health

Word Form Chart

NOUN	VERB	ADJECTIVE	ADVERB
autopsy	autopsy		
		cardiac	
cast			
checkup			
clinic		clinical	clinically
contagion		contagious	
		critical	critically
crutch			
fracture	fracture	fractured	
inflammation	inflame	inflamed	
		intensive	intensively
joint	join	joined	
outpatient		outpatient	
paramedic			
pediatrician		pediatric	
pediatrics			
prevention	prevent	preventive	preventively
side effect			
special	specialize	specialized	
specialization			
specialist			
sprain	sprain	sprained	
stabilization	stabilize	stable	
sterilization	sterilize	sterile	
transfusion	transfuse		
tumor			

Definitions and Examples

1. **autopsy,** n. [a medical examination of a dead body to determine the cause of death]

   From the autopsy results, the medical examiners determined that a sudden heart attack killed the man.

   The autopsy showed that the girl died from food poisoning.

2. **cardiac,** adj. [related to the heart]

   My grandfather had cardiac surgery to repair a hole in the wall of his heart.

   The cardiac care unit is on the fifth floor of the hospital.

3. **cast,** n. [a hard shell used to protect broken bones while they heal]

   I had to wear a cast on my leg for six weeks after I broke it in a skiing accident.

   The little girl didn't want to wear the cast on her broken arm, but the doctors told her she had to.

4. **checkup,** n. [a visit to the doctor to examine someone's general health, not for any specific health problem]

   Many doctors recommend that adults have a checkup once a year.

   Newborn babies go in for checkups quite often during the first few months of life.

5. **clinic,** n. [a medical center, usually smaller than a hospital but larger than a doctor's office]

   Our town is too small to have a hospital, but it does have a good clinic.

   Alcoholics often go to a substance abuse clinic to get help to stop drinking.

6. **contagious,** adj. [able to be spread to another person]

   The flu is a contagious disease.

   If you are very careful about washing your hands, you are less likely to get contagious diseases.

7. **critical,** adj. [dangerous; in a very serious or dangerous condition]

   My cousin's husband is a critical care nurse who works with patients recovering from heart surgery.

   My neighbor is critically ill with cancer and unlikely to survive more than a few weeks.

8. **crutch,** n. [a supporting device usually fitting under the arms that people with injured legs use to help themselves walk]

I'll be on crutches for five weeks until my broken ankle heals.

Nowadays, crutches are often made of aluminum because it is a metal that is strong but light.

9. **fracture,** v.t. [to break or crack, especially a bone]

Thomas fractured his arm playing soccer.

Fractures heal much faster in small children than in older adults.

10. **inflame,** v. [to become red and swollen, usually because of injury or infection]

I got such a bad sunburn that the skin on my face and chest became inflamed, and I had to see a dermatologist.

My husband's appendix was so inflamed that it would have burst soon if the doctors hadn't removed it.

11. **intensive,** adj. [very concentrated and thorough]

Ann is undergoing intensive treatment with antibiotics to cure her lung infection.

After major surgery, many patients stay in the intensive care unit for at least several hours.

12. **joint,** n. [a part of the skeleton where two or more bones come together]

My elbows and other joints often ache after I exercise.

Athletes can injure their knee joints because they run so much.

13. **outpatient,** n. [a patient who is treated at a hospital and then sent home that same day without staying overnight]

The clinic handles only outpatients who are able to go home the day of their surgery.

Thanks to laser surgery, many kinds of minor operations are done on an outpatient basis.

14. **paramedic,** n. [a person trained in emergency medical procedures]

The ambulance service is staffed with three paramedics who can handle any medical emergency.

Firefighters are also qualified to serve as paramedics.

15. **pediatric,** adj. [having to do with children]

   This children's hospital is a nationally known pediatric center.

   After working as a general practitioner for three years, Roberta continued her medical studies in order to become a pediatrician.

16. **preventive,** adj. [designed to keep medical problems from happening]

   Many family doctors put a lot of emphasis on preventive medicine to keep their patients as healthy as possible.

   Preventive medicine focuses on eating healthy foods, exercising, and dealing with life stress in a positive way.

17. **side effect,** n. [a secondary consequence of taking a medication, often uncomfortable or even dangerous]

   One side effect of many allergy medicines is a very dry mouth.

   A doctor or pharmacist should always explain possible side effects of medicines to patients.

18. **specialist,** n. [a doctor who has studied to be an expert in one particular kind of illness or one kind of patient; a person who is an expert in one area]

   A general practitioner can treat basic medical problems, but she will often send her patients to a specialist for extended treatment by an expert.

   A dermatologist is a specialist who treats skin problems.

19. **sprain,** v.t. [to injure by twisting or pulling]

   Heather was lucky that she only sprained her ankle instead of breaking it when she fell.

   A sprained shoulder is a very painful injury.

20. **stable,** adj. [a term to describe a patient who is conscious and in no immediate danger but who is still uncomfortable and who may yet have medical complications]

   John's medical condition is now stable, so he will be moved out of the critical care unit and into a regular room.

   The first thing paramedics will do to an injured person is to stop any major bleeding and otherwise stabilize him.

21. **sterile,** adj. [completely free from any germs]

    It is extremely important to maintain sterile conditions in the operating room.

    Most surgical supplies come in sterile packaging.

22. **transfusion,** n. [putting blood that has been collected from one person into another person]

    The accident victim lost so much blood that he needed an emergency transfusion.

    In the early 1980s, some patients got AIDS because they received blood transfusions from infected people.

23. **tumor,** n. [a group of cells that divides and spreads too fast, as in cancer]

    She had a tumor on her liver that had to be surgically removed.

    The tumor had spread from his intestines to his stomach before it was discovered.

Exercises

A. Match each word or phrase with its definition or synonym.

_____ 1. paramedic	a.	putting donated blood into a person for medical reasons
_____ 2. autopsy	b.	a mass of cells that grows out of control
_____ 3. clinic	c.	a doctor who is an expert in one specific area
_____ 4. crutch	d.	a routine examination of one's general health
_____ 5. transfusion	e.	a break or crack
_____ 6. inflamed	f.	a result of taking a medicine other than the result that is intended
_____ 7. joint	g.	a medical office, smaller than a hospital
_____ 8. specialist	h.	an examination of a dead body to decide what killed the person
_____ 9. side effect	i.	a place where two bones meet, like the elbow or knee

_____ 10. checkup   j. a device that people with injured legs use to walk

_____ 11. tumor   k. red and swollen

_____ 12. fracture   l. a medical worker trained in emergency procedures

B. Answer each question with a word or phrase from the word form chart. Use the correct form of the word or phrase in your answer.

1. What do doctors give someone who loses a lot of blood suddenly and needs more blood?_____

2. If you break your arm, what do you wear on it while the bones heal?

   _____

3. What kind of medicine focuses on keeping a person healthy?

   _____

4. What do you lean on for help in walking if you break your leg?

   _____

5. What does one call doctors who work only with children?

   _____

6. What do we call the procedure of examining a dead body to learn the cause of death?_____

7. What is the term that describes elbows, knees, wrists, and ankles?

   _____

8. Which term refers to pure, clean, and germ-free?

   _____

9. What hospital unit does a dangerously sick person stay in? (two possible answers)_____

10. What is another word for a break in a bone? _____

C. Circle the correct answers. Some questions will have more than one correct answer.

1. Which one(s) would most people think of as being useful?

   a. side effect   b. paramedic   c. inflammation   d. checkup   e. tumor

2. Which one(s) might be found in a person's body?

   a. tumor   b. crutch   c. cast   d. clinic   e. fracture

3. Which one(s) might a doctor do or make?

   a. crutch   b. transfusion   c. paramedic   d. outpatient   e. autopsy

4. Which one(s) can help people who are recovering from an illness or accident?

   a. side effect   b. cast   c. inflammation   d. crutch   e. fracture

5. Which one(s) describe people?

   a. pediatrician   b. transfusion   c. paramedic   d. autopsy   e. specialist

D. Write *T* if the sentence is true and *F* if it is false.

_____ 1. The common cold is not contagious.

_____ 2. The stomach is a cardiac organ.

_____ 3. If your condition is stable after surgery, that is a good sign that you will be fine.

_____ 4. Doctors and nurses do not work at clinics.

_____ 5. A fracture is not caused by a virus.

_____ 6. Patients in the critical care unit of a hospital require extra attention from the nursing staff.

_____ 7. Critical injuries are usually treated on an outpatient basis.

_____ 8. A fracture is treated with antibiotics.

_____ 9. If you sprain your ankle, you will find it almost impossible to walk.

_____ 10. A side effect is meant to be the most important effect that a medicine has on a person.

E. Complete each analogy with a word or phrase from the word form chart.

1. _____ : blood :: vaccination : vaccine

2. tree : bush :: hospital : _____

3. knee : _____ :: cat : animal

4. automotive : car :: _____ : heart

5. firefighter : fire engine :: _____ : ambulance

6. antibiotics : infection :: cast : _____

7. dirty : _____ :: noisy : silent

8. _____ : specialist :: bus : vehicle

F. Circle the word that is least related in meaning to the others.

1. inflamed	sterile	clean
2. cast	tumor	crutch
3. checkup	prevention	outpatient
4. side effect	pediatrician	specialist
5. sprain	paramedic	fracture
6. contagious	stable	steady
7. transfusion	hospital	clinic

G. Read the passage. Then, in each blank, write the most appropriate word or phrase from the word form chart. Use the correct form of the word or phrase. Some items may be used more than once.

The staff of a large emergency room has to be ready for anything. In many large cities, (1) _____ bring patients to hospital emergency rooms suffering from bullet wounds, knife wounds, and severe injuries from automobile accidents. Usually the ambulance staff has already (2) _____ the patient, so that she or he is no longer in any immediate danger. Then the doctors can evaluate the patient and see what has to be done. They may need to perform a blood (3) _____ if the person has been bleeding a lot. Sometimes they have to call in a

(4) _____ for a complicated case. For example, if

the patient's heart is injured, a (5) _____ surgeon

may have to operate. To treat a child who is seriously injured, a

(6) _____ may be consulted. Of course, not all

emergency room patients are (7) _____ injured. Many

suffer from less dramatic injuries, such as a (8) _____

ankle or a (9) _____ bone, which require X rays and

either a special bandage or a (10)_____, and often

(11) _____ so that the person will be able to walk

around.

   Many emergency rooms spend too much time treating patients who should

actually be treated in a doctor's office or a (12) _____,

leaving the emergency room free to handle the true emergencies. An average

(13) _____ offers very different services from an

emergency room. People can go there for a (14)_____,

to see how their general health is. They can also get some information on

staying healthy, since clinics have more time and resources to focus on

(15) _____ medicine. When doctors

at a clinic prescribe a medicine, they take the time to go over any possible

(16) _____ so that the patient knows what to ex-

pect. The doctors or nurses at a clinic also give vaccinations to children to keep

them from getting some of the more common childhood diseases, and they handle

common bacterial infections, such as ear infections, with antibiotics. In addition

they advise patients on how to treat standard viral diseases, such as the common

cold or the flu. They may have patients with ongoing problems, such as rheumatoid

arthritis, a very painful (17)_____ of the

(18) _____. Some clinics can even perform simple

surgeries on an (19) _____ basis, so that the patient

can recover at home the same day as the surgery.

Collocations

1. **autopsy**—perform an autopsy; conduct an autopsy; carry out an autopsy; autopsy results; autopsy report

2. **cardiac**—suffer a cardiac arrest; cardiac care; cardiac death; cardiac equipment; cardiac massage; cardiac pacemaker; cardiac seizure; cardiac surgery; cardiac unit; cardiac stress

3. **cast**—plaster cast; place a cast on; remove a cast; wear a cast

4. **checkup**—regular checkup; yearly checkup; medical checkup; routine checkup; annual checkup

5. **clinic**—family clinic; hospital clinic; private clinic; local clinic; rehabilitation clinic; outpatient clinic; sports clinic; veterinary clinic

6. **contagious**—highly contagious; contagious disease; contagious enthusiasm; contagious outbreak

7. **critical**—critical illness; critical care; listed in critical condition; on the critical list

8. **crutches**—require crutches; emotional crutch; hobble on crutches

9. **fracture**—multiple fracture; stress fracture; hairline fracture; bone fracture; compound fracture; skull fracture

10. **inflamed**—swollen and inflamed; irritated and inflamed; inflamed joints; inflamed tissue

11. **intensive**—intensive care; under intensive care; intensive care unit; neonatal intensive care; intensive research; intensive negotiations; labor intensive

12. **joint**—stiff joint; painful joint; aching joints

13. **outpatient**—inpatient and outpatient; on an outpatient basis; outpatient clinic; outpatient department; outpatient treatment; outpatient care; outpatient services; outpatient therapy

14. **paramedic**—paramedic equipment; paramedic team; paramedic training

15. **pediatric**—pediatric center; pediatric clinic; pediatric nurse; pediatric services; pediatric trauma unit; pediatric visit

16. **preventive**—preventive medicine; preventive health care; preventive measures; preventive action; preventive approach

17. **side effect**—frequent side effect; common side effect; negative side effect; little-known side effect; related side effect; unfortunate side effect; potentially serious side effect; commonly noted side effect

18. **specialist**—leading specialist in his/her field; cardiac specialist; consult a specialist; refer someone to a specialist

19. **sprain**—bad sprain; sprained ankle; sprained wrist

20. **stable**—stable condition; stabilize the patient

21. **sterile**—sterile procedure; sterile dressing; sterile needles; sterile pad; sterile bandage; sterile equipment; sterile environment; sterile solution

22. **transfusion**—emergency transfusion; blood transfusion

23. **tumor**—malignant tumor; benign tumor; brain tumor; tumor cells; tumor growth; inoperable tumor

Exercises

H. (a) **Circle the word or phrase that frequently collocates with the word in boldface. Refer to the collocations list. The first one is an example.**

(b) **Write a sentence using the collocation formed by the circled word or phrase and the word in boldface. Underline the collocation. The first one is an example.**

1. **side effect**   yearly   (common)   complete

   A common side effect of many medications is an upset stomach.

2. **joints**   annual   aching   human

   _____

   _____

3. **intensive**   care unit   relief   ambulance

   _____

   _____

4. **fracture**   disabled   chosen   compound

_____

_____

5. **contagious**   highly   individually   shortly

_____

_____

6. **clinic**   usual   entertaining   local

_____

_____

7. **checkup**   yearly   malignant   long

_____

_____

8. **pediatric**   pharmacist   parent   nurse

_____

_____

9. **sprained**   nose   ankle   ear

_____

_____

I. Complete the following sentences by using a collocation from the list below. If necessary, change the form of the words in the collocation to fit the sentence. The first one is an example.

emergency transfusion	listed in critical condition
cardiac arrest	hobble on crutches
autopsy report	benign tumor
plaster cast	outpatient therapy
preventive approach	sterile procedures

1. The hospital has George ___listed in critical condition___ as he is still dangerously sick.

2. Many health care professionals prefer to take a(n) _____, which focuses on helping patients maintain a healthy lifestyle so that they do not develop health problems.

3. The police won't know what killed the man until they receive a(n) _____ from the medical examiner's office.

4. His grandfather went into _____, but the paramedics got his heart beating again.

5. It is extremely important to maintain _____ in the operating room so that the equipment does not become contaminated and cause infections.

6. He'll be _____ for about a month, because he fractured both legs.

7. I will be able to recover from my knee surgery at home with the help of some _____ four times a week.

8. It was a(n) _____, so the surgeons didn't remove it. As long as it doesn't grow, it shouldn't cause any harm.

9. He lost so much blood in the accident that the doctors had to perform a(n) _____.

10. They put a(n) _____ around the girl's broken wrist so she wouldn't break it again before it healed.

Discussion or Writing

J. Answer the following questions.

1. How valuable do you think preventive medicine is? Why do many health professionals feel it is a good idea to get a yearly checkup?

2. Have you ever been on crutches? What are some of the difficulties facing a person on crutches?

3. Today surgeons can do many operations on an outpatient basis that used to require a hospital stay. What are some of the benefits of this change?

4. What are some of the more common contagious diseases? How can they be prevented?

5. Why can it sometimes be important to perform an autopsy?

Language

Word Form Chart

NOUN	VERB	ADJECTIVE	ADVERB
alternative	alternate	alternative	alternatively
analogy		analogous	analogously
anecdote		anecdotal	anecdotally
anticlimax		anticlimactic	anticlimactically
articulation	articulate	articulate	articulately
attribute	attribute	attributable	
classic		classic	classically
		classical	
colloquialism		colloquial	colloquially
connotation	connote	connotative	
copyright	copyright		
criticism		critical	critically
critique	critique		
distinction	distinguish	distinguishable	
figure of speech		figurative	figuratively
genre			
inspiration	inspire	inspiring	inspirationally
		inspired	
		inspirational	
irony		ironical	ironically
		ironic	
lucidity		lucid	lucidly
omniscience		omniscient	omnisciently
pathos		pathetic	pathetically
proverb		proverbial	proverbially
realism		realistic	realistically
response	respond	responsive	responsively
satire	satirize	satirical	satirically
		viable	

Definitions and Examples

1. **alternative,** n. [a choice between two or more; another choice]

   James had two alternatives: to take either the course on Shakespeare's comedies or the course on the modern novel.

   I can take a flight from Seoul directly to Hawaii; alternatively, I can fly from Seoul to Tokyo, stop over for some sight-seeing, and then go on to Hawaii.

2. **analogy,** n. [a comparison using a familiar thing to explain something else]

   Professor Wilson drew an analogy between countries going to war and children fighting in a school playground.

   Learning a language and learning to play the piano are analogous since both involve physical movement and production of sound, but they are different in many other ways.

3. **anecdote,** n. [a story about an interesting or amusing event]

   A famous radio show is based on anecdotes about fictional people who live in a fictional place named Lake Wobegon.

   Anecdotal reports about human behavior cannot substitute for controlled psychological experiments based on scientific principles.

4. **anticlimax,** n. [a conclusion that is surprisingly weak, especially when a strong or dramatic ending is expected]

   The play was very exciting, but its ending was an anticlimax.

   We were made to believe that the negotiations would end with a real peace treaty, but the outcome was an anticlimactic statement about continuing the discussions at some future date.

5. **articulate,** adj. [able to express oneself in words easily and clearly]

   When he speaks in public, Troy is always articulate and fluent.

   It can be difficult to articulate what you are thinking if you are trying to express complex ideas.

6. **(a) attribute,** n. [a quality or characteristic]

   Good literature has two special attributes: interesting ideas and excellent, expressive language.

   (b) attribute, v. [to say that something is the cause]

   Her great poetry is attributed to her unusual life experience and her amazing ability to say much in a few well-chosen words.

7. **(a) classic,** n. [a famous work of excellent and lasting quality]

   Dante's *Inferno* is a literary classic.

   (b) classic, adj. [perfectly typical]

   The play recently staged in Paris is a classic example of modern theater.

8. **colloquial,** adj. [having the quality of informal, spoken language]

   Colloquial language is not used in an academic paper.

   In a movie, colloquialisms are frequently used in the dialogue.

9. **connotation,** n. [the meaning that a word may have in addition to its explicit or "dictionary" meaning]

   The journalist chose words with negative connotations to report on the speeches of the politicians whom she disliked.

   The word *mother* literally means "female parent," but for many people it also connotes love, caring, and security.

10. **copyright,** n. [the legal ownership of a creative work; the legal right to control sales of written work, music, and other material]

    Copyright laws vary from one country to another, so it often happens that an artist's work is legally protected in one country but copied freely in another.

    Copyrighted publications usually have the copyright owner's name on the title page.

11. **(a) critical,** adj. [having the quality of a careful analysis or evaluation]

    After a critical assessment of the library, Dr. O'Reilly reported to the committee that its services were excellent.

    (b) critical, adj. [having a tendency to make negative judgments]

    Professor Michaels is so critical of the written work of his students that some try to avoid taking his courses.

12. **distinguish,** v. [to see the differences between things]

   It is not easy to distinguish fact from fiction in essays that are a mix of autobiography and imagination.

   The styles of these two authors are so similar that they are not easily distinguishable.

13. **figure of speech,** n. [a description that uses words in an unusual way or compares different things in order to create a more vivid picture in the mind of the reader or listener]

   Sports writers used various figures of speech to describe Michael Jordan's performance on the basketball court, such as "He flies through the air like a bird!" and "When Michael jumps, he touches the sky and the hearts of the fans!"

   Figurative language is very important in literature, especially in poetry.

14. **genre,** n. [a specific type or kind, often used in reference to literary or artistic works]

   Students of literature are introduced to many different genres, such as drama, poetry, novels, fiction, and nonfiction.

   Some examples of popular film genres are horror, action, and romance movies.

15. **inspire,** v. [to have a stimulating effect; to assist in making someone more creative]

   Theater or movie directors try to inspire confidence in actors to help them perform as well as possible.

   It is said that much of a writer's inspiration comes from his or her own life.

16. **irony,** n. [a way of using words to express meaning that is the opposite of or different from the literal or usual meaning, often for a sarcastic purpose; a situation or an action that is strangely different from the expected one]

   Comedians often use irony to make people laugh, as, for example, when they ask a quiet, dull audience, "Why are you all so happy and lively?"

   It was ironic that Lee received a speeding ticket because he was the one who was always telling people to drive slowly and carefully.

17. **lucid,** adj. [clear; easy to understand]

   The students enjoy Professor Sobiso's lectures since they are always lucid.

   The author of the textbook *An Introduction to Biotechnology* explains all the new concepts very lucidly.

18. **omniscient,** adj. [having complete knowledge of everything]

> Novels are sometimes written from the point of view of an imagined, all-knowing person who is the omniscient narrator.

> In various religious traditions, there is the belief in a god whose main characteristic is omniscience, and the same being is also considered omnipresent and omnipotent.

19. **pathetic,** n. [having the characteristic of making a person feel pity or sadness]

> The young actress was brilliant in her performance as a pathetic, lost child.

> There was great pathos in the way the man quietly asked for money or food to help his family.

20. **proverb,** n. [a brief, well-known statement expressing popular wisdom or advice]

> Proverbs or traditional wise sayings are found in every language.

> Many cultures have parallel proverbial expressions because they are based on universal human experiences, for example, the English proverb *More haste, less speed* and the Somali proverb *He who takes his time does not fall.*

21. **realistic,** adj. [having the quality of showing things or people as they actually are; giving an accurate picture; practical]

> Some artists create very realistic paintings, while others prefer to be more abstract.

> Realistically speaking, a person cannot become a successful professional without the appropriate training, experience, and hard work.

22. **respond,** v. [to react to an influence; to reply]

> If you respond to a question with silence, that is itself a kind of reply.

> Everyone responded positively to the new policies proposed by the government.

23. **satire,** n. [the use of irony, humor, or ridicule to criticize something foolish or harmful]

> The novel is a social satire focusing on people whose only concern is to succeed in business and make lots of money.

> At the Byham Theater last week, I saw a wonderful satirical comedy that made fun of the corrupt behavior of some senior politicians.

24. viable, adj. [workable; capable of being used; likely to develop in a successful manner]

> Rodrigo's plan is a viable way of getting the job done.

> Because of your job and family responsibilities, there is only one viable option for you—to be a part-time student taking most of your courses in the evening.

Exercises

A. Match each word with its definition or synonym.

___ 1. anecdotal	a.	make fun of or ridicule
___ 2. connotation	b.	related to casual speaking style
___ 3. critique	c.	having meaning opposite to the literal one
___ 4. ironical	d.	arousing pity
___ 5. proverb	e.	meaning indirectly associated with a word
___ 6. respond	f.	a popular wise saying
___ 7. satirize	g.	stimulating creativity
___ 8. viable	h.	like a brief story
___ 9. pathetic	i.	careful analysis and evaluation
___ 10. analogy	j.	type of comparison
___ 11. colloquial	k.	that is likely to work
___ 12. inspirational	l.	react to an influence or question

B. Answer each question with a word or phrase from the word form chart. Use the correct form of the word or phrase in your answer.

1. What does one have when there are two or more possibilities to choose from?

   _____

2. What do we call specific types or styles of communication such as poetry, journalism, and academic writing? _____

3. What type of description, often found in poetry, uses comparisons of things that are not normally considered similar, in order to make the description more effective?_____

4. If someone knows everything, what would you call that person?

_____

5. How would you describe items that you can tell apart?_____

6. What is a common expression expressing popular wisdom or advice?

_____

7. If someone is describing something in a way that is easy to comprehend, how is it being described?_____

C. Complete each sentence with a word or phrase from the word form chart. Use the correct form in your answer.

1. An unexpectedly weak ending is _____.

2. Ownership of a written or artistic work is called _____.

3. A(n) _____ example of something is one that follows the exact format of its type.

4. A person who is fluent and effective in language use speaks and writes

_____.

5. If I say that X is the cause of Y, I am _____ Y to X.

6. A lifelike, exact picture of something is a(n) _____ one.

D. Write *T* if the sentence is true and *F* if it is false.

____ 1. Inspirational words make people unhappy.

____ 2. A classical work of art is never appreciated by art lovers.

____ 3. Informal, spoken language uses colloquial expressions.

____ 4. A pathetic anecdote can make you sad.

____ 5. An articulate person uses language effectively.

___ 6. Genres are general arguments.

___ 7. An ironical statement should be understood literally.

___ 8. A plan that might work out well is viable.

___ 9. Figures of speech often compare things that are different to provide an effective description.

___ 10. An alternative allows only one possibility.

E. Circle the word that is least related in meaning to the others.

1. alternate   critique   evaluation

2. distinguishable   impressive   separable

3. analogy   comparison   description

4. response   reply   return

5. satirize   support   ridicule

6. realistically   seriously   accurately

7. explicit   connotative   implied

8. omniscient   all-knowing   brilliant

9. manner   attribute   quality

10. proverbial   traditional   contemporary

11. anticlimactically satirically   ineffectively

12. connotation   copyright   ownership

F. An incomplete sentence is given at the beginning of this exercise. Each item will complete the sentence in a different way. In each blank, write the most appropriate word or phrase from the choices given in parentheses. Use the correct forms of the words. The first one is an example.

Incomplete sentence

Various language strategies and argumentative techniques are available if you want to influence the opinions of others; for example, you could . . .

Different ways to complete the sentence

1. ... use _satire_ (satire, speech) to mock something you think is foolish.

2. ... make _____ (ironic, particular) comments, such as, "How clever he was to steal the money! It landed him in jail."

3. ... choose words with specific _____ (aspects, connotations) to affect the listener indirectly, such as *guerrilla* or *freedom fighter* or *terrorist* to refer to a rebel fighter.

4. ... use an _____ (attitude, analogy) to clarify a concept.

5. ... tell a(n) _____ (anecdote, lie) to express an idea, like the one about the traveler who asks everyone the way to his destination and changes his route frequently—thus never reaching the destination.

6. ... use the _____ (classic, circular) forms of argument—induction and deduction—to make your point logically.

7. ... say that your position is supported by someone who is _____ (omniscient, adequate).

8. ... be very _____ (critical of, sympathetic to) any arguments that do not support your own view, pointing out all their weaknesses.

9. ... _____ (present, attribute) negative characteristics to the people who oppose you.

10. ... mention some _____ (promises, proverbs) because many people are impressed by their underlying popular wisdom.

11. ... _____ (realistically, classically) describe the bad consequences that might follow if the listener or reader does not agree with you.

12. ... make your opponents realize that their plans would not be _____ (copyrighted, viable) in actual practice.

G. Complete each analogy with a word or phrase from the word form chart.

1. _____ : let down :: genre : kind

2. literal : implied :: formal : _____

3. obey : command :: _____ : question

4. _____ : pity :: humor : laugh

5. drawing : pictures :: _____ : words

6. story : anecdote :: choice : _____

7. _____ : confusion :: peace : disturbance

H. In your own words, explain the main idea of each sentence.

1. I could not distinguish one twin from the other.

2. Figuratively speaking, Shakespeare, compared to all other dramatists, is a giant oak tree among small plants.

3. Large corporations often pay inspirational speakers to motivate their employees.

4. Violating copyright could lead to a fine or jail time.

Collocations

1. **alternative**—possible alternative; only one alternative; many alternatives; choose an alternative; provide alternatives; cheaper alternative; consider alternatives

2. **analogy**—analogy between; make an analogy; draw an analogy; analogous situation; analogous to; false analogy

3. **anecdote**—anecdotal information; anecdotal evidence; anecdotal testimony; tell an anecdote; recount an anecdote; amusing anecdote; funny anecdote

4. **anticlimax**—conclude anticlimactically; end anticlimactically; anticlimactic conclusion; anticlimactic ending

5. **articulate**—articulate speaker; clear articulation; unclear articulation; highly articulate

6. **attribute**—desirable attribute; essential attribute; human attribute; personal attribute; attribute to

7. **classic**—classic style; classic case; classic design; classic symptoms; modern classic; pop classic

8. **colloquial**—colloquial expression; colloquial words; colloquial speech; colloquial language

9. **connotation**—positive connotation; negative connotation

10. **copyright**—copyrighted material; copyright laws; violate copyright; copyright agreement

11. **critical**—highly critical; critical acclaim; critical analysis; critical evaluation; critical assessment; sharp criticism

12. **distinguish**—clearly distinguishable; easily distinguishable; barely distinguishable; hardly distinguishable

13. **figure of speech**—not just a figure of speech; effective figure of speech; figurative expression; figurative language; figuratively speaking

14. **genre**—new genre; film genre; literary genre; musical genre; popular genre; crime genre

15. **inspire**—inspire confidence; inspire enthusiasm; inspire pride; provide inspiration; give inspiration; divine inspiration; flash of inspiration

16. **irony**—ironic(al) statement; speaking ironically; a hint of irony; subtle irony; dramatic irony

17. **lucid**—lucid analysis; lucid explanation; lucid presentation; lucid style; describe lucidly

18. **omniscient**—omniscient god; omniscient narrator; omniscient and omnipotent; omniscient and omnipresent

19. **pathetic**—pathetic sight; pathetic attempt; pathetic cries; pathetic drama; moments of pathos; heartfelt pathos

20. **proverb**—an old proverb; as the proverb goes; quote a proverb; as the proverb says; familiar proverb; proverbial expressions

21. **realistic**—realistic idea; realistic expectation; realistic view; realistic portrayal; artistic realism; pictorial realism; a sense of realism

22. **respond**—respond positively; respond negatively; sensitive response; respond to treatment; respond to questions; respond promptly; respond to a demand

23. **satire**—political satire; social satire; strong satire; sharp satire; biting satire; funny satire; gentle satire; satirical humor; satirical cartoon; satirical tone

24. **viable**—viable proposition; viable tool; viable idea; viable alternative; economically viable; financially viable; viable solution

Exercises

I. **Complete the following sentences by using a collocation from the list below. Use the correct form of the collocation to fit the sentence. The first one is an example.**

omniscient god	flash of inspiration	personal attribute
clear articulation	popular genre	not just a figure of speech
economically viable	copyrighted material	speak ironically

1. Maria's ___clear articulation___ ensured that she was always understood when she gave a speech.

2. The anthropologist discovered that the group she was studying included a(n) _____ among their religious beliefs.

3. Henry said it was _____ to say that his brother was as intelligent as Albert Einstein; he really thinks his brother is one of the world's greatest geniuses.

4. Theater and film are _____ of entertainment in my city, but I prefer to stay at home and read a good novel.

5. Two of the _____ needed by successful politicians are the power of persuasion and the ability to get things done for the people whom they represent.

6. The football coach was joking and _____ when he said that his team would win the competition easily; he knew that they had no chance of success.

7. There is no _____ plan for constructing a new City Hall because the city's budget never has extra funds for such large projects.

8. Professor McDougall had struggled for many months to find a solution to the mathematical problem and had almost given up when the solution came to her in a(n) _____.

9. Laws concerning _____ vary a lot from one country to another, but in general they legally protect intellectual property such as written work, art, and computer software.

J. **In each of the following sentences, part of a collocation is underlined and part of it is missing. Complete each sentence by writing the missing part of the collocation in the blank. Use the correct form of the words in the collocation to fit the sentence. The first one is an example.**

1. Neddy Seagoon always keeps us laughing by telling us (a) <u>amusing anecdotes</u>, and some of his stories include (b) <u>satirical</u> <u>humor</u> that makes fun of politicians.

2. "Don't count your chickens before they hatch" and "The grass is always greener on the other side" are <u>familiar</u> English _____.

3. The doctor said that I was suffering from a (a) _____ <u>case</u> of pneumonia because I had all the usual symptoms including fever, chest pain, difficulty breathing, and coughing, but fortunately I (b) _____ well <u>to treatment</u> at home and did not have to go to the hospital.

4. It is normal to use _____ <u>words and expressions</u> when speaking to friends but not when writing a formal report.

5. The _____ <u>cries</u> of the lost child were finally heard by someone who had been sent to look for him.

6. Most people thought that the painting of the queen was a _____ <u>portrayal</u>, but the king disagreed, saying that she was much more beautiful than the painting showed.

K. **(a) Circle the word that frequently collocates with the word in boldface. Refer to the collocations list. The first one is an example.**

(b) Write a sentence using the collocation formed by the circled word or phrase and the word in boldface. Underline the collocation. The first one is an example.

1. **alternatives**   speak   (consider)   behave

   You should <u>consider</u> all <u>alternatives</u> before you make important career decisions.

2. **critical**   highly   anecdotally   proverbially

   _____

   _____

3. **attribute**   to   at   from

   _____

   _____

4. **connotation**   total   proper   negative

   _____

   _____

5. **distinguishable**   barely   critically   intelligently

   _____

   _____

6. **anticlimactically**   begin   continue   conclude

_____

_____

7. **explanation**   lucid   funny   connotative

_____

_____

8. **analogous**   by   to   against

_____

_____

Discussion or Writing

L. **The following proverbs all refer to the use of language.**

(a) Discuss the meaning of each proverb, giving examples to show why it may or may not be true.

(b) Do you know another proverb, in any language, that refers to the use of language? If so, explain its meaning and say why it may or may not be true.

1. Love understands all languages. (Romanian)

2. Do not use words that are too big for your mouth. (Iranian)

3. To speak ill of anyone is to speak ill of yourself. (Afghan)

4. Wisdom consists of ten parts—nine parts of silence and one part with few words. (Arabic)

5. Even the best words bring no food. (Gambian)

6. Friendly words are convincing. (Indian)

7. The pen is mightier than the sword. (English)

8. A picture is worth ten thousand words. (Chinese)

9. Polite words open iron gates. (Croatian)

10. All food is fit to eat, but not all words are fit to speak. (Haitian)

11. When deeds speak, words are nothing. (Xhosa)

12. The punishment of a liar is that he is never believed, even when he speaks the truth. (Hebrew)

Life Science

Word Form Chart

NOUN	VERB	ADJECTIVE	ADVERB
antibody			
bacteriologist		bacteriological	
bacteriology			
bacterium		bacterial	
compound		compound	
comprise			
convergence	converge	convergent	
degeneration	degenerate	degenerate	
		degenerative	
derivative	derive	derivative	derivatively
divergence	diverge	divergent	divergently
	embed	embedded	
	encompass		
heredity	inherit	hereditary	
hormone		hormonal	hormonally
hybrid	hybridize	hybrid	
hybridization			
immunity	immunize	immune	
		immunized	
immunization			
immunology			
microscope		microscopic	microscopically
organism			
parasite	parasitize	parasitic	parasitically
reproduction	reproduce	reproductive	reproductively
respiration	respire	respiratory	
secretion	secrete	secreted	
stimulus	stimulate	stimulating	
		stimulated	
vaccine	vaccinate	vaccinated	
vaccination			
virus		viral	

Definitions and Examples

1. **antibody,** n. [a protein substance in the blood, sometimes formed in reaction to invading germs for protection against disease]

   Because the sick child's blood did not contain the needed antibodies, she died of the disease.

   Vaccination stimulates the immune system to create antibodies against specific diseases.

2. **bacterium,** n. {pl. **bacteria**} [single-celled organisms, some of which cause disease]

   Louis Pasteur discovered that some harmful bacteria can be destroyed by heat.

   Bacterial infections can be treated with antibiotics such as penicillin.

3. **compound,** adj. [made of parts that are connected in an orderly way]

   The compound leaf was made of several smaller parts connected to a stalk in pairs.

   A chemical compound contains more than one element.

4. **comprise,** v.t. [to include]

   The plant comprises the roots, stalk, leaves, and the male and female parts of the flower.

   The university's graduate program is comprised of a medical school, a law school, a business school, and several other specialized courses of study.

5. **converge,** v.i. [to come closer together or become more similar]

   The two cars converged at high speed but avoided hitting each other at the last second.

   Scientists explain the similarity of structure in the wings of birds and flying insects by the theory of convergence or "convergent evolution."

6. **degenerate,** v.i. [to become lower in quality]

   The quality of the furniture produced by the factory degenerated when it hired workers with less experience and training.

   A person suffering from a degenerative disease becomes sicker as time goes on.

7. derive, v.t. [to obtain something from a source, or to come from a source]

People can derive pleasure from accomplishing a difficult task.

If writing music or playing an instrument is a basic art form, then conducting an orchestra is a derivative kind of art.

8. diverge, v.i. [to move farther apart; to become less similar]

Robert Frost, in a well-known poem, wrote "two roads diverged in a yellow wood," and his decision to follow one of them and not the other made a great difference in his life.

Two members of the same family may have divergent opinions, even if their parents tried to teach them the same values.

9. embed, v.t. [to fix or set something into a different material that holds it in place]

The bricks in the path were embedded in cement and could not be moved.

The doctor will embed a device in her arm to prevent conception for the next three years.

10. encompass, v.t. [to surround on all sides, to contain]

The chain-link fence encompasses the elementary school, the play area, and the soccer field.

In the country on moonless nights, we feel encompassed by blackness.

11. heredity, n. [the biological characteristics that an organism obtains from its parents; the biological processes through which these characteristics are passed on]

Is heredity or environment more important in determining a person's success and happiness in life?

If two people plan to marry, it is a good idea for them to find out if there are any hereditary diseases in their families.

12. hormone, n. [a secretion which turns on, turns off, or regulates a process within an organism and which can exert its effect in a location in the body distant from where it was produced]

The tiny boy was given hormone treatments to make him grow taller.

Hormonal imbalances can make people sick.

13. **hybrid,** n. [a cross between, or mixture of, two species or varieties]

    Some hybrids are stronger than either parent, but some are sterile.

    Hybridization has produced food crops with desirable traits from both parent varieties.

14. **immune,** adj. [resistant to negative effects, such as diseases]

    Before traveling, it is important to obtain inoculations to make one immune to diseases that might be present in the new environment.

    Immunity to certain common diseases is a characteristic of some hybrid grains.

15. **microscope,** n. [a scientific instrument that permits the user to see very small objects like bacteria by greatly magnifying them]

    Objects which are so small that we need a microscope to see them are called microscopic.

    Medical technicians microscopically examine blood samples to try to detect signs of disease.

16. **organism,** n. [a living being]

    A microorganism is an organism of microscopic size.

    Giant redwood trees, people, fish, and bacteria are organisms.

17. **parasite,** n. [an organism which obtains nourishment or other vital substances from another living organism without providing any help to that other organism]

    People can get some parasitic diseases by drinking unclean water or eating incompletely cooked food.

    A parasite does not live independently.

18. **reproduction,** n. [the process of making more of the same type of thing or organism]

    A single organism can live without reproducing, but a species must be capable of reproduction or it will die out.

    Scientists often try to reproduce natural processes in the laboratory in order to study them in a controlled setting.

19. **respiration,** n. [breathing; within cells, the process of obtaining usable energy from simple sugar; the exchange of gases within an organism that allows this energy to be used]

> The emergency medical technicians gave the drowning victim artificial respiration until she was put on a respirator in the hospital.

> Organisms that cannot respire cannot live.

20. **secretion,** n. [the production in a cell or body part of a substance having a specific job to do in an organism; the substance produced by this process]

> The hormones that regulate growth are secretions.

> Saliva, secreted in the mouth, begins the process of digestion.

21. **stimulus,** n. {pl. **stimuli**} [something that causes an organism or part of it to begin to work or to work more efficiently]

> We may react to stimuli such as noise or caffeine differently depending on our health, mood, and personality.

> The light that shines in our windows in the morning stimulates us to wake up.

22. **vaccine,** n. [a substance which will stimulate an immunity against a given disease]

> Before children may begin school in the United States, they must be vaccinated against several childhood diseases.

> Researchers are trying to develop an AIDS vaccine.

23. **virus,** n. [a microorganism that can live only within certain cells and that is too small to be seen under an ordinary light microscope; a microorganism that can cause disease in animals and plants]

> Polio and influenza are viral diseases.

> A virus can be dormant for long periods of time, and then it can begin to act like a living organism again when its environment is right for growth and reproduction.

Exercises

A. Match each word with its definition or synonym.

___ 1. comprise   a. turn on or start

___ 2. derive   b. obtain from

___ 3. embed   c. breathe

___ 4. stimulate   d. put in

___ 5. respire   e. include

B. Circle the correct answers. Some questions will have more than one correct answer.

1. Which are alive?

     a. parasites   b. organisms   c. bacteria   d. hybrids

2. Which are processes?

     a. stimulus   b. divergence   c. respiration   d. vaccine

3. Which are always very small?

     a. organisms   b. viruses   c. antibodies   d. hybrids

4. Which are fields of study that biologists may be interested in?

     a. microscopes   b. compound   c. embedding   d. heredity

5. Which can cause disease?

     a. viruses   b. bacteria   c. parasites   d. prognoses

6. Which can protect against disease?

     a. degeneration   b. derivative   c. vaccines   d. antibodies

7. Which are things that can be produced by living organisms?

     a. reproduction   b. hybrids   c. secretions   d. hormones

8. Which can describe something's form, structure, or size?

    a. parasitic   b. compound   c. stimulated   d. microscopic

9. Which are processes related to heredity?

    a. reproduction   b. hybridization   c. respiration   d. secretion

10. Which can describe people?

    a. diverse   b. microscopic   c. secreted   d. immune

C. Write *T* if the sentence is true and *F* if it is false.

____ 1. To stimulate something is to make a model of it.

____ 2. Hybrids have two parents that are unlike in some way.

____ 3. Vaccination can produce immunity to some diseases.

____ 4. Species that converge become more similar to each other than they were before.

____ 5. A secretion is a kind of hormone.

____ 6. The diverse species in an environment can be categorized.

____ 7. Respiration stops when a sick person dies.

____ 8. A parasite lives independently, without deriving any benefits from other organisms.

____ 9. A compound structure comprises several parts.

D. Circle the word that is least related in meaning to the others.

1. surrounded   embedded   divergent

2. include   forget   encompass

3. heredity   antibody   genetics

4. secretion   microscope   hormone

5. bacterium   microorganism   hybrid

6. degenerative   viral   bacterial

E. Complete each analogy with a word from the word form chart.

1. _____ : single :: many : one

2. _____ : divergence :: together : apart

3. _____ : secretion :: bread : food

4. immunity : _____ :: knowledge : education

5. comprise : include :: _____ : set into

6. _____ : microorganism :: telescope : stars

7. _____ : add :: die : subtract

8. bacterium : disease :: _____ : sickness

9. _____ : on :: extinguish : off

10. _____ : pure :: mixed : homogeneous

11. grow : shrink :: _____ : improve

12. _____ : surround :: uncover : reveal

F. Answer each question with a word from the word form chart. Use the correct form of the word in your answer.

1. What do we call an organism that lives within or on another and steals from it? _____

2. What is a microscopic part of the immune system? _____

3. How do we get tears and hormones? _____

4. What is the general term for something that lives? _____

5. What must an organism do to stay alive? _____

6. When you put something inside something else, so that it stays in place, what are you doing? _____

7. What are we doing when we get something from a source? _____

8. What must a species do to avoid dying out? _____

G. **In each blank, write the most appropriate word from the list given after each sentence. Some words may be used more than once. Use the correct form of the word.**

1. To _____ the _____ system to produce _____ against a _____ or _____ disease, a doctor will _____ the patient.

   immune   bacterial   virus   vaccination   stimulate   antibodies

2. _____ of living organisms comprise _____ and many other fluids.

   hormones   secrete

3. Over a long period of time, changes in species may _____ or _____, and instead of improving these species may _____, depending on the environment.

   degenerate   convergent   divergence

4. The set of all _____ _____ microorganisms and many other, larger, living creatures.

   comprise   organism

5. _____ _____ some characteristics of both parents, but, because the parents are of _____ types, the offspring often cannot _____.

   diverge   hybrids   inherit   reproduction

6. We need a _____ to see _____ made of single cells, such as _____, and we need special _____ to see very small microorganisms, such as viruses, which have no cells at all.

   bacterial   microscope   organism

H. Complete the crossword puzzle using words from the word form chart. One answer has been given.

Across

2. put in and keep in place, inside
3. a mixed species
5. what starts or enhances a process
6. to get from something
8. surrounded
10. a special kind of secretion
12. a dependent organism
14. get worse
15. a very small life-form
16. to take in and use oxygen
18. a living thing
20. not simple in structure
21. very small
22. many small organisms that may cause disease

Down

1. genetic inheritance
4. resistant
7. preventive medicines
9. to approach each other
10. pronoun for single male
11. to make more of a kind
13. part of the immune system
14. different; growing apart
17. consist of
19. This is produced by an organism.

Collocations

1. **bacterium**—aerobic bacteria, anaerobic bacteria; bacterial infection; bacterial disease; bacteriological weapon; bacteriological warfare

2. **compound**—compound structure; compound form; chemical compound; compound eye; compound leaf

3. **comprise**—be comprised of; comprises several; comprises a large number of

4. **converge**—convergence of; converge with; convergent evolution

5. **degenerate**—degenerate into; degenerative disease

6. **derived**—derived form; derived from

7. **diverge**—divergent views; divergent opinions; divergent paths

8. **encompass**—encompassed by; all-encompassing

9. **heredity**—hereditary disease; hereditary characteristic; heredity versus environment

10. **hormone**—hormone therapy; hormone replacement; sex hormone; growth hormone; male hormones; female hormones; synthetic hormones; hormonal imbalance

11. **hybrid**—hybrid form; hybrid seed; hybrid vigor

12. **immunity**—natural immunity; immune deficiency; immune system; immune response; immune to; immunize against; immunization record

13. **microscope**—microscopic form; electron microscope; light microscope; oil-immersion microscope

14. **organism**—living organism

15. **parasite**—parasitic disease; intestinal parasite; human parasite

16. **reproduce**—reproductive capacity; reproductive ability; reproductive system; reproductive choice

17. **respire**—artificial respiration; aerobic respiration; anaerobic respiration; respiration rate; respiratory arrest; respiratory failure; upper respiratory infection

18. **stimulus**—strong stimulus; weak stimulus; stimulus and response; provide a stimulus for

19. **vaccine**—HIV, AIDS vaccine; smallpox vaccine; vaccination record

20. **virus**—viral infection; viral disease; polio virus; flu virus; AIDS virus; viral pneumonia

Exercises

I. (a) **In each list of words below, underline every word that frequently collocates with the word in boldface. The first one is an example.**

(b) **Write a sentence using one of the collocations formed in part a. In your sentences, use the correct forms of the words in the collocation and underline the collocation. The first one is an example.**

1. **bacteria**   virus   <u>infection</u>   <u>aerobic</u>   degenerate

   _____ The bacterial infection caused a high fever. _____

2. **stimulus**   response   vaccine   disease   converge

   _____

   _____

3. **respiration**   infection   reproduction   rate   artificial

   _____

   _____

4. **virus**   AIDS   encompassed   compound   convergent

   _____

   _____

5. **hormone**   rate   replacement   vaccination   therapy

   _____

   _____

J. Replace the underlined parts of each sentence with a complete collocation from the collocations list. Part of the collocation is provided in boldface. In the blank, write the rest of the collocation. The first one is an example.

1. For every <u>action or substance that acts as a cause,</u> there is at least one <u>effect or consequence.</u>

    Answer: **stimulus** . . . <u>response</u>

2. According to the doctor, my cousin has <u>an illness caused by a microorganism.</u>

    Answer: a _____ **infection**

3. Plant biologists tell us that <u>the special strength of mixed forms</u> is the reason that many new food crops grow so well.

    Answer: **hybrid** _____

4. Many researchers are looking for <u>something that will stimulate immunity against a serious sexually transmitted disease caused by a very small microorganism.</u>

    Answer: an **AIDS** _____

5. In order to avoid making mistakes in classification, a biologist must know a lot about <u>how different species change and develop similar structures when they have similar survival needs.</u>

    Answer: _____ **evolution**

6. She is not likely to recover because she has <u>an illness which makes her body weaker and less efficient, day by day.</u>

    Answer: a _____ **disease**

7. Medical people can use machinery to save a person who is in <u>a state of not breathing.</u>

    Answer: **respiratory** _____

8. Some older people are given <u>medical treatment with special human secretions that they no longer make enough of themselves.</u>

    Answer: _____ **replacement** _____

9. <u>What protects the body against disease</u> comprises many parts, including the skin, special cells in the blood, antibodies, etc.

Answer: the _____ **system**

10. Some say that to predict a person's future success, one must look at both his or her education and <u>the important characteristics from his or her parents.</u>

Answer: **his/her** _____ **influences**

11. Without regular exercise, even an athlete can <u>get weaker and less fit, and become</u> a "couch potato."

Answer: _____ **into**

Discussion or Writing

K. Answer the following questions.

1. Is heredity or environment more important in determining behavior? Give reasons for your answer.

2. What kinds of diseases can people get, and how can they protect themselves against disease? How can doctors help them to protect themselves?

3. How can the study of heredity benefit humanity? How about the study of immunology?

4. How do we recognize that something is a living organism?

Politics

Word Form Chart

NOUN	VERB	ADJECTIVE	ADVERB
agitation	agitate	agitated	
agitator			
allotment	allot	allotted	
amnesty			
anarchy		anarchic	anarchically
aristocracy		aristocratic	aristocratically
aristocrat			
boycott	boycott		
canvass	canvass		
canvasser			
constituency	constitute		
constituent			
dictator	dictate	dictatorial	dictatorially
dictatorship			
encounter	encounter		
federation	federate	federal	
		forthcoming	
impeachment	impeach		
institute	institute	institutional	
institution	institutionalize		
mandate	mandate	mandatory	
monarch			
monarchy			
scenario			
secession	secede		
		so-called	
sovereign		sovereign	
sovereignty			
statesman		statesmanlike	statesmanly

NOUN	VERB	ADJECTIVE	ADVERB
tyranny tyrant veto	tyrannize veto	totalitarian tyrannical	tyrannically

Definitions and Examples

1. **agitate,** v.t. [to stir up people by arguing publicly in favor of change; to disturb or excite]

    In some countries, political agitators are not tolerated; they may be thrown into jail.

    Maria noticed a lot of agitation among the office staff when she arrived at work, and she soon heard that a burglar had broken into the building during the night and taken valuable items.

2. **allot,** v.t. [to distribute; to assign]

    In some political systems, each part of the country is allotted a number of government representatives in proportion to its population.

    Our allotment of furniture and office supplies arrived in time for us to get ready to receive our first clients.

3. **amnesty,** n. [a general pardoning of crimes, most often in relation to political offenses]

    Thirty-eight detainees were freed in the amnesty which followed the change of regime.

    A one-month amnesty period was granted during which illegally owned guns could be handed over to the police without punishment and without questions being asked.

4. **anarchy,** n. [a state of disorder, confusion, and violence due to lack of effective government]

> After the assassination of the president, there was a brief period of anarchy before order was restored by the army.

> The president's advisers said that there would be anarchy if he did not approve the strict new laws against large public gatherings of protesters.

5. **aristocracy,** n. [a class of people who have a high position in society because of their birth or inherited wealth and rank]

> Democratic revolutions, like the French Revolution in 1789, often remove aristocracies from power.

> Aristocratic attitudes of superiority are not usually appreciated.

6. **boycott,** n. [a refusal to deal with or buy from a person or group in order to punish or force a change of behavior]

> The boycott of products made by Jayson Corporation, called as a protest against its policy of using low-paid, nonunion workers, greatly reduced its profits.

> So many citizens boycotted the city's public transportation system when prices were raised that the prices were soon lowered again.

7. **canvass,** v.t. [to get information or support by going from person to person and asking questions or persuading them]

> Politicians frequently canvass their constituents to gather opinions on current issues.

> Before elections, it is common to see canvassers going from door to door talking to residents and giving them political campaign literature.

8. **constituency,** n. [a group of citizens who can elect representatives to government positions; a group of supporters]

> Our congressman is often in contact with his constituency and is therefore very popular with us.

> Hector Lawson ran for office to reform education, but he had no constituency of teachers to help him in his efforts.

9. **dictatorship,** n. [a type of government in which power is held by one person or a small group]

> Most people do not enjoy living in a dictatorship.

> A dictator may have to use force to make people obey.

10. **encounter,** n. [a meeting between people that is usually unexpected and often difficult]

> The mayor had several encounters with rival politicians at public meetings during the election campaign.

> Dictators use force and threats to get their own way when they encounter people who criticize their policies.

11. **federation,** n. [a form of government or organization in which power is shared by a central authority and a group of states, regions, countries, or associations that come together to form a larger unit of organization]

> A federation will work well only as long as the states involved have a common purpose.

> As a consequence of years of exploitation by mine owners, several coal miners' associations formed a union called the Colliery Workers Federation.

12. **forthcoming,** adj. [about to happen fairly soon]

> The forthcoming announcement of an amnesty is being eagerly awaited by many prisoners.

> The tourists were given a list of forthcoming cultural and entertainment events to choose from.

13. **impeach,** v.t. [to officially charge a public official with misconduct in office]

> It is unusual for a president to be impeached, and even more unusual for a president to be impeached and removed from office or imprisoned.

> A campaign to impeach Mr. Donaldson for lying to Parliament gained only a few supporters.

14. **institution,** n. [an official organization that supports a special activity or function]

> The University of Pittsburgh is a famous institution of higher learning.

> The city council decided to institutionalize and unite into one organization all the charities and unofficial groups that were providing help to needy people.

15. mandate, n. [an order or a command given by an authority; the power to do something authorized by a government or by the vote of the people]

A mandate to enroll all voters was issued by the Supreme Court.

The mayor said that he had been mandated by the citizens to change the way the city police operated.

16. monarchy, n. [a type of government in which the ruler is a king or a queen or an emperor]

The monarch of Great Britain is the most famous in the world.

According to republicans, all monarchies should be abolished or have only a ceremonial function.

17. scenario, n. [an imagined situation; a set of circumstances that has not yet happened]

The government official gave three different scenarios for how the terrorists might attack.

A likely scenario for the result of the election is that the Liberal Party will again lose to the Conservative Party.

18. secede, v.i. [to officially leave an organization, usually in reference to groups of people, regions, or countries]

The secession of one state from the union caused a chain reaction, and others soon also broke away.

The Conservative Party members have said that they will secede from the coalition government if some of their policies are not adopted.

19. so-called, adj. [incorrectly referred to; not really what something appears to be]

The so-called army was in fact several groups of citizens who had had very little training.

Tourists are often cheated by so-called guides who wait at airports and offer to show them around.

20. sovereignty, n. [supreme power, especially that of a monarch]

The queen's sovereignty included her own country and many other lands that were part of her great empire.

A sovereign state is one which has full control over all its affairs, without interference from any other.

21. **statesman,** n. [a person who conducts government affairs at a high level or internationally and who is recognized and respected for doing so wisely and honorably]

The secretary-general of the United Nations has to be a wise statesman.

The prime minister's statesmanlike handling of the crisis impressed everyone, including his enemies.

22. **totalitarian,** adj. [having complete control over all aspects of citizens' lives and usually keeping such control by force]

Democratic and totalitarian countries are opposites of each other.

Strong armies and force are typically used by totalitarian regimes to maintain power.

23. **tyrant,** n. [a ruler who has complete power that is usually maintained by force and who uses the power in strict or cruel ways]

Alexander the Great, Hitler, and Mussolini are often described as tyrants.

A leader whose behavior is tyrannical soon loses the confidence and respect of his followers.

24. **veto,** v.t. [to officially refuse to accept a policy or behavior]

The chair of the committee has veto power over any decisions that she does not like.

When the mayor vetoed the suggested new law, she angered many citizens.

Exercises

A. Match each word with its definition or synonym.

_____ 1. allot   a. organization with a special function

_____ 2. anarchy   b. ruler with complete control, often applied in cruel ways

_____ 3. agitate   c. leave an organization

_____ 4. constituency d. supreme power

_____ 5. statesman   e. distribute

_____ 6. institution   f. having complete control of all aspects of life and government

_____ 7. monarchy   g. a senior and wise government official

_____ 8. secede   h. cause a disturbance

_____ 9. sovereignty   i. disorder and confusion

_____ 10. totalitarian   j. government by a king or queen

_____ 11. tyrant   k. group of supporters or voters

B. Answer each question with a word or phrase from the word form chart. Use the correct form of the word or phrase in your answer.

1. What is declared when many offenders are forgiven at the same time?

   _____

2. If you make people upset, angry, and excited what are you doing to them?

   _____

3. What does one call people who have high rank in society due to the families they are born into? _____

4. When a group of people refuse to buy from a company, what are they doing?

   _____

5. How would we describe a president of a country who successfully negotiates fair international treaties with other countries? _____

6. How would one describe a system of government or a ruler with absolute power?_____

7. What are you doing if you walk from house to house along a street, trying to get the people to vote for the candidate that you support?

   _____

8. What is the word for a group of countries or associations that get together to form one larger unit while still keeping some powers in the hands of the separate units? _____

9. If a public official is guilty of a crime, what might be the consequence?

_____

10. When an official authority gives a command for something to be done, what is it called? _____

11. How may we describe something that we believe is not really what it claims to be?_____

12. What is the term for the official power to reject a proposal?

_____

C. Circle the correct answers. Some questions will have more than one correct answer.

1. Which are not persons?

    a. dictator   b. encounter   c. tyrant   d. canvasser   e. veto   f. sovereign

2. Which are systems of government?

    a. scenario   b. monarchy   c. dictatorship   d. mandate
    e. statesman   f. federation

3. Which could be a positive result of cooperation between governments or associations?

    a. encounter   b. forthcoming   c. anarchy   d. federation
    e. tyranny   f. agitation

4. Which can describe a person's characteristics?

    a. mandatory   b. dictatorial   c. statesmanly   d. institutional   e. federal

5. Which are actions that can be done by one person?

    a. allot   b. debate   c. impeach   d. tyrannize   e. veto   f. federate

D. Write *T* if the sentence is true and *F* if it is false.

____ 1. People like to be allotted at least their fair share of good things.

____ 2. Anarchic behavior in the classroom will make the instructor happy.

___ 3. An encounter occurs when you part from people.

___ 4. A person in a constituency has no say in electing its representative.

___ 5. Dictators are often disliked by those under them.

___ 6. Canvassers force others to agree with them.

___ 7. A school is an example of an institution.

___ 8. Princes and princesses are monarchs.

___ 9. Secession from an association means becoming completely independent of it.

___ 10. A king is a sovereign.

___ 11. A totalitarian regime allows the people of the country to decide most things for themselves.

___ 12. Tyrants are pleasant and gentle toward their citizens.

E. Complete each analogy with a word or phrase from the word form chart.

1. _____ : force :: democracy : vote

2. correct : incorrect :: real : _____

3. king : _____ :: president : leader

4. previous : past :: _____ : future

5. _____ : secede :: join : separate

6. institution : hospital :: _____: princess

F. Circle the word that is least related in meaning.

1. dictatorial	totalitarian	anarchic
2. amnesty	imprisonment	freedom
3. impeach	charge	allot
4. constituent	whole	entirety
5. mandate	command	permit
6. sovereign	ruler	agitator
7. tyrant	aristocrat	dictator
8. constituency	dictatorship	monarchy

G. In each blank, write the appropriate word from the list below. Use each word only once. Use the correct form of the word.

boycott	forthcoming	allot	mandatory
anarchy	sovereign	statesmanlike	institutionalize

1. When politicians do not behave honorably toward their citizens or in relations with other countries, the citizens usually realize it quite easily. By contrast, when high government officials behave in a _____ manner, the citizens are likely to support them in any _____ elections and negotiations.

2. In many countries, government welfare supports those who are unable to find work or who cannot work because of disabilities. The help is _____ according to need. Usually such payments are made without expectation of anything in exchange, but sometimes it is _____ that the recipient do some work in return for the help. The informal term *workfare* (from *welfare* and *work*) has been invented to refer to this required work.

3. During the civil rights movement in the United States in the 1960s, _____ were effectively used in an attempt to influence businesses and city governments that discriminated against African Americans. The financial losses caused many businesses and city services, such as public transportation, to change their _____ racist policies.

Collocations

1. **agitation**—agitate against; agitate for; civil agitation; social agitation; political agitation; nationalist agitation; political agitators; outside agitators

2. **allot**—allot to; allot equal amounts; fair allotment; unfair allotment

3. **amnesty**—general amnesty; declare an amnesty; government amnesty; offer amnesty to; Amnesty International

4. **anarchy**—civil anarchy; political anarchy; social anarchy; general anarchy; risk of anarchy; anarchy and lawlessness; sink into anarchy; plunge into anarchy

5. **aristocracy**—member of the aristocracy; royalty and aristocracy; social aristocracy; aristocratic manner

6. **boycott**—economic boycott; threaten a boycott against; impose a boycott

7. **canvass**—canvass people's opinions; canvass people's views; canvass door-to-door; political canvasser

8. **constituency**—represent a constituency; voters in a constituency; national constituency; local constituency

9. **dictatorship**—military dictatorship; violent dictatorship; brutal dictatorship

10. **encounter**—have an encounter; encounter obstacles; brief encounter; encounter problems; chance encounter; unexpected encounter

11. **federation**—members of a federation; international federation; break up a federation

12. **forthcoming**—forthcoming elections; forthcoming summit; forthcoming attractions; forthcoming trip; forthcoming event

13. **impeach**—grounds for impeachment; impeachment vote

14. **institution**—institutionalized policy; institutional framework; institutional authority; ruling institution; research institution; professional institution; educational institute

15. **mandate**—seek a mandate from; have a mandate from

16. **monarchy**—hereditary monarchy; constitutional monarchy

17. **scenario**—worst-case scenario; best-case scenario; likely scenario; possible scenario; probable scenario; unlikely scenario; nightmare scenario; credible scenario

18. **secede**—secede from a federation; secede from a union; threaten to secede; have a right to secede; decide to secede

19. **so-called**—so-called friends; so-called supporters; so-called freedom

20. **sovereignty**—declare sovereignty; national sovereignty; sovereign nation

21. **statesman**—wise statesman; respected statesman; elder statesman; international statesman; statesmanlike behavior

22. **totalitarian**—totalitarian regime; totalitarian government; totalitarian rule; totalitarian society; totalitarian system

23. **tyrant**—wicked tyrant; bloody tyrant; tyrannical oppression; evil tyranny

24. **veto**—override a veto; threaten a veto; have the power of veto

Exercises

H. Complete the following sentences by using a collocation from the list below. Use the correct forms of the words in the collocation to fit the sentence. The first one is an example.

member of the aristocracy	declare an amnesty
fall into anarchy	allot equally to
impose a boycott	best-case scenario
military dictatorship	canvass opinions
seek a mandate from	statesmanlike behavior
national sovereignty	tyrannical behavior
threaten a veto	

1. Portions of food were _allotted equally to_ the hungry refugees.

2. After the earthquake, there was no governmental control and the country _____.

3. The boss's _____ caused much fear among his employees.

4. When the parliament did not agree with him, the president usually tried to _____ the people themselves through a vote.

5. The president _____ to try to stop the Senate from passing laws he did not like.

6. As a well-known _____, Lord Pickering had a lot of influence with the king and queen.

7. The political prisoners were very happy when the new government _____ and they were released.

8. Violation of _____ can sometimes lead to war.

9. If one country _____ on products from another country, a trade war might start.

10. Tyrants and dictators do not normally demonstrate _____ in dealing with their own people or foreign governments.

11. The _____ is that everyone in the country will agree with all aspects of the new policy and not argue over it only to achieve personal goals.

12. _____ are very often overthrown in coups led by other soldiers.

13. Politicians often _____ of citizens before proposing legislation that will affect many people.

I. (a) **Circle the word or phrase that frequently collocates with the word in boldface. Refer to the collocations list. The first one is an example.**

(b) **Write a sentence using the collocation formed by the circled word or phrase and the word in boldface. Underline the collocation. The first one is an example.**

1. **anarchy**   fruitful   departure from   (risk of)

   Following the assassination of the president, there was a risk of anarchy, so

   the army was called to patrol the streets of the capital.

2. **agitator**   statesmanlike   sovereign   political

   _____

   _____

3. **constituency**   claims   voters   victories

   _____

   _____

4. **statesman**   respected   hated   local

   _____

   _____

5. **federation**   intercept   total   international

   _____

   _____

6. **impeachment**	allotment to	aristocracy	grounds for

_____

_____

7. **institution**	complete	research	divide into

_____

_____

8. **monarchy**	hereditary	committee	purpose

_____

_____

9. **secede**	union	apparatus	fail

_____

_____

10. **totalitarian**	addition	completion	rule

_____

_____

11. **tyranny**	sweet	evil	enjoyable

_____

_____

J. Complete the sentence by circling the letter of the word or phrase that collocates with the word in boldface. The first one is an example.

1. While canvassing door to door, the candidate, Mr. Lee, was surprised by a(n) _____ **encounter** with one of his political rivals.

   a. mandatory   b. unexpected

2. A series of unpopular decisions by the parliament led to _____
agitation.

   a. civil   b. comparable

3. The king's _____ **supporters** deserted him in the end.

   a. social   b. so-called

4. **Canvassing** consumers' _____ is essential before designing an
advertising campaign.

   a. abilities   b. opinions

5. Some of the _____ **events** for children are games, movies, and a
puppet show.

   a. forthcoming   b. careful

Discussion or Writing

K. Answer the following questions.

1. Have you ever been in any place where there was anarchy? If so what was the
place and situation? How did you feel about it?

2. Should countries be ruled by aristocracies? Why or why not?

3. In what situations is it appropriate to impeach a national leader?

4. Have you ever had veto power over other peoples' decisions? If so, describe the
situation.

Psychology

Word Form Chart

NOUN	VERB	ADJECTIVE	ADVERB
alienation	alienate	alienating	
		alienated	
bias	bias	biased	
delusion	delude	delusional	delusionally
		deluded	
deviation	deviate	deviant	deviantly
disclosure	disclose	disclosed	
disparity		disparate	disparately
ego		egotistical	egotistically
		egoistic	
hypnosis	hypnotize	hypnotic	hypnotically
		hypnotizing	
		hypnotized	
insomnia		insomniac	
insomniac			
intellect			
intellectual		intellectual	intellectually
		interpersonal	interpersonally
merger	merge	merging	
		merged	
mind-set			
morale			
network	network	networking	
		networked	
networking			
outlook			
		primal	
procrastinator	procrastinate	procrastinating	
procrastination			

NOUN	VERB	ADJECTIVE	ADVERB
reconstruction scrutiny sentiment syndrome	reconstruct scrutinize	reconstructive sentimental subliminal	reconstructively sentimentally subliminally

Definitions and Examples

1. **alienate,** v.t. [to make someone who is part of a group feel separate from the group]

   The club alienated one of its members when it publicly accused him of attending meetings without paying dues.

   Jonas felt alienated when his friend did not invite him to the birthday party.

2. **bias,** n. [a preference that influences one's decisions or judgments]

   Judy's bias for blue is exemplified in her choice of clothes; every suit that she buys is a shade of blue.

   When asked to choose between the two applicants for the job, Ms. Michaels said she could not be involved in the decision because her friendship with one of the applicants made her biased.

3. **delusion,** n. [a false belief, often one that is held in spite of evidence against it; self-deception; belief that something is true only because one wants it to be true]

   He was under the delusion that the project could not be done without him, so he was quite surprised when he was asked to stop working on it.

   We thought she was delusional when she said she would complete her degree in two years instead of three, but she actually achieved her goal.

4. **deviation,** n. [a change from something expected or accepted]

   Any small deviation from the planned route would get them lost.

   Children may deviate from the career path that their parents would choose for them.

5. **disclose,** v.t. [to make information publicly known]

> The union did not disclose the details of the new contract until all the union members had been informed.

> The disclosure of the patient's personal information was a violation of her rights to privacy.

6. **disparate,** adj. [fundamentally different; unlike]

> Disparate groups often unite when faced with a common enemy.

> When the company was forced to reveal its pay scales for all workers, the disparity between women's salaries and men's salaries was noticeable.

7. **ego,** n. [the self; one's sense of oneself; one's opinion of oneself]

> We joked that his ego was so big that he would not be able to fit through doorways any more.

> John is egotistical and opinionated, and he never gives serious consideration to other people's feelings or ideas.

8. **hypnosis,** n. [a sleeplike state during which a person can be influenced or controlled by the suggestions of others]

> Hypnosis is a tool used by some psychotherapists in treating their patients.

> Some people try to quit smoking through suggestions given to them in a hypnotic state.

9. **insomnia,** n. [an inability to sleep even though one wants to]

> Insomnia can sometimes be attributed to stress, anxiety, or depression.

> My neighbor is an insomniac, so she sometimes gets out of bed in the middle of the night and cleans her house, after which she finds she can easily fall asleep.

10. **intellect,** n. [the ability to think and gain knowledge]

> In politics, great intellect is not enough to get elected; great personal appeal is needed.

> Her superior intellect helped her win the academic scholarship.

11. **interpersonal,** adj. [about relationships between people]

   A teenager may be more concerned about interpersonal problems than academic problems.

   People with good interpersonal skills are hired by companies to work in personnel offices because their work focuses on supporting the staff.

12. **merger,** n. [the joining of two organizations or companies to form a larger one]

   The merger of the two companies resulted in 103 employees losing their jobs.

   With so few members, we cannot get any funding from the university, so our student organization needs to merge with another one.

13. **mind-set,** n. [a fixed attitude; an established mental inclination]

   Having a positive mind-set can help one find a solution to a difficult problem.

   Sachi's thinking did not fit the company's mind-set, so she soon began to search for another job.

14. **morale,** n. [a person or group's level of positive or negative attitude]

   After half of the employees were fired, the morale of the remaining employees was very low.

   The coach's main job was to keep up the players' morale because their confidence and enthusiasm were fading after they lost five games in a row.

15. **networking,** n. [connecting to or exchanging information with others for work-related or social purposes]

   He views every major social event that he attends as an opportunity for networking to improve his career opportunities.

   After ten years in the company, she had built an excellent network of business contacts.

16. **outlook,** n. [a perspective; a point of view]

   People who have a positive outlook on life enjoy life more.

   A series of happy events can improve a person's outlook on life.

17. **primal,** adj. [very basic; early in development]

    Fear is considered a primal emotion in humans.

    A primal urge or instinct of living creatures is to find food.

18. **procrastinate,** v.i. [to delay in doing something that should be done]

    I often use an excuse like cleaning my bedroom as a way to procrastinate when I have to write a research paper.

    If you do not stop procrastinating, you'll never get the business report done in time!

19. **reconstruct,** v.t. [to rebuild; to make over]

    After the monument was destroyed during the war, the citizens worked to reconstruct it.

    A country must work toward economic reconstruction following an economic crisis.

20. **scrutinize,** v.t. [to examine something very carefully, with attention to detail]

    Due to the difficulty of diagnosis of this case, the doctors will have to scrutinize all the patient's medical test results and records for information that might help them understand her illness.

    Passport control officers usually scrutinize immigration documents.

21. **sentiment,** n. [a feeling about something that influences one's opinions or thoughts]

    The public sentiment toward the city's mayor changed when they learned he had cheated on his city taxes.

    Sentimental movies always make me cry.

22. **subliminal,** adj. [functioning at a subconscious level so that one is not fully aware of it]

    Advertisements often try to use subliminal messages to get shoppers to buy more.

    Although people do not always realize the impact of a significant piece of literature when they read it, they may feel the effect at a subliminal level.

23. **syndrome,** n. [a group of signs or symptoms that indicate a particular problem or disease]

    There are four stages in the "battered woman syndrome": denial, guilt, enlightenment, and responsibility.

    Although the term "acquired immune deficiency syndrome" is common in articles and the news, most people recognize the acronym *AIDS* more easily.

Exercises

A. Match each word with its definition or synonym.

___	1. delusion	a.	attitude
___	2. intellect	b.	join
___	3. scrutinize	c.	self-deception
___	4. disparate	d.	sleeplessness
___	5. bias	e.	look at very closely
___	6. mind-set	f.	perspective
___	7. procrastinate	g.	preference
___	8. insomnia	h.	basic
___	9. primal	i.	intelligence
___	10. reconstruct	j.	delay
___	11. outlook	k.	rebuild
___	12. merge	l.	different

B. Answer each question with a word from the word form chart. Use the correct form of the word in your answer.

1. How would you feel if your friends stopped talking to you?_____

2. How might we describe movies or stories that make us cry?_____

3. How can you increase the number of people you know in businesses or fields related to yours? _____

4. What kind of communication skills are important when one has to talk to people often as part of a job? _____

5. If someone has a particular set of medical symptoms, what might they indicate that the person is suffering from? _____

6. What psychotherapy technique might help someone remember the forgotten details of an event experienced many years earlier? _____

7. What are you doing if you tell someone's secrets to others?_____

8. If employees are feeling stressed and negative about their work, what should their employer try to improve?_____

C. **Indicate the grammatical function of each word in the list. A word can have more than one grammatical function. Use these abbreviations:**

N = noun   V = verb   ADJ = adjective   ADV = adverb

The first one is an example.

ADV 1. interpersonally

_____ 2. alienate   _____ 9. disclosure

_____ 3. biased   _____ 10. subliminally

_____ 4. delude   _____ 11. procrastinate

_____ 5. egotistical   _____ 12. intellectually

_____ 6. hypnotic   _____ 13. disparity

_____ 7. deviation   _____ 14. reconstructive

_____ 8. network   _____ 15. scrutinize

D. **Write *T* if the sentence is true, and *F* if it is false.**

___ 1. If you follow the same path as everyone else, you are deviating from the path.

___ 2. Someone with a big ego usually thinks everyone else is better.

___ 3. If you experience subliminal messages about snacks and drinks while at the movies, you might decide that you are hungry without knowing why.

___ 4. Scrutinizing your work closely often means that you do not care about it.

_____ 5. Insomniacs might try homemade remedies like warm milk or herbal tea to help them sleep.

_____ 6. Reading books and attending classes can help someone learn primal instincts.

_____ 7. A biased opinion is not free of individual beliefs or feelings.

_____ 8. Successfully merging two people's ideas is an example that supports the saying "two heads are better than one."

E. Circle the word that is least related in meaning to the others.

1. disclose	withhold	retain	keep
2. disparity	heterogeneity	same	different
3. rehearse	remake	rebuild	reconstruct
4. primal	learned	ancient	primitive
5. intellectual	smart	dumb	intelligent
6. hurry	procrastinate	speed	quicken
7. deviate	differ	vary	conform
8. fact	emotion	feeling	sentiment

F. In each blank, write the most appropriate word from the list below. Use the correct form of the word. Some words in the list will not be used.

merging	biased	scrutinizing	interpersonal
outlook	alienated	subliminal	disparate
reconstruction	morale	delusions	insomnia

The expression "man's best friend" has come to mean more than just a good pet. When we get home from work or school, dogs are always happy to see us, which is a real boost for our (1)_____. Beyond the common benefits, however, dogs have been providing service to humans for centuries. Various methods of using dogs to help people have been implemented. For instance, seeing-eye dogs help people who are blind. Some dogs are trained to work with people in wheelchairs, constantly monitoring their needs and helping them retrieve items or carry items. Others are trained to assist police officers who are (2)_____ suspicious packages that may contain drugs or explosives. In addition to providing tangible support, dogs can supply emotional support. Therapists who work with abused children may bring specially trained dogs into the therapy sessions as a bridge to help the child with (3)_____ relationships. The children may feel (4)_____ from people, but they often respond positively to animals. Some elderly persons benefit from owning a dog because it helps them maintain a positive (5)_____ on life. For instance, they can get outdoor exercise by walking the dog and have a sense of being needed. If they suffer from (6)_____, the dog may help them not feel alone when they are awake at night. These are only a few examples of ways in which humankind's best friends are currently at work. In the street, in the home, or in the therapist's office, dogs offer love and service.

G. Complete the crossword puzzle using words from the word form chart.

Across
1. about relationships between people
9. feeling
10. joining
11. detailed examination
13. ability to think
15. movement away from the expected route
16. system of connections
17. unlike
19. point of view
21. sleeplike state in which one is influenced by suggestions
22. attitude

Down
1. sleeplessness
2. self
3. delay
4. functioning at a subconscious level
5. make someone feel no longer part of something
6. tell
7. self-deception
8. basic
12. rebuild
14. positive or negative attitude
18. disease indicated by symptoms
20. preference

Collocations

1. **alienate**—alienation from; alienation of

2. **bias**—bias against; bias toward; gender bias; political bias; religious bias; cultural bias; personal bias

3. **delusion**—self-delusion; under the delusion; under no delusion; suffering from the delusion

4. **deviation**—deviation from the norm; sharp deviation; deviant behavior

5. **disclose**—refuse to disclose; fail to disclose; failure to disclose; unwilling to disclose; disclose details; disclose information

6. **disparate**—disparate settings; disparate elements; disparate cultures; highly disparate; great disparity in; wide disparity between

7. **ego**—male ego; big ego; inflated ego; flatter someone's ego; ego boost; be on an ego trip (colloquial)

8. **hypnosis**—self-hypnosis; put someone under hypnosis; be under hypnosis; deep hypnosis

9. **insomnia**—suffer from insomnia; chronic insomnia; temporary insomnia

10. **intellect**—keen intellect; great intellect; brilliant intellect; superior intellect; human intellect; person of keen intellect; sharpen one's intellect

11. **interpersonal**—interpersonal skills; interpersonal relationships; interpersonal experiences; interpersonal problems

12. **merger**—merge gradually; carry out a merger between X and Y; reject the merger with X; agree to the merger with Y; merge with; merger of X and Y

13. **mind-set**—negative mind-set; positive mind-set; proper mind-set; be of a particular mind-set

14. **morale**—morale boost; low morale; sagging morale; high morale; lift morale; improve morale; destroy morale; morale is at rock bottom

15. **network**—support network; old-boy network; old-girl network; network of informants; nationwide network; worldwide network

16. **outlook**—positive outlook on; have a positive outlook; have a negative outlook; outlook for the future

17. **primal**—primal origins; primal fear; primal instincts; primal qualities

18. **procrastinate**—keep on procrastinating; stop procrastinating

19. **reconstruct**—reconstruct the events; reconstruct the economy; reconstruct history

20. **scrutinize**—closely scrutinize; carefully scrutinize; scrutinize the details; subject something to careful scrutiny; under scrutiny

21. **sentiment**—express a sentiment; growing sentiment; strong sentiment; sentiment against; sentiment for; show sentiment

22. **subliminal**—subliminal advertising; subliminal message; at a subliminal level; on a subliminal level

23. **syndrome**—points to a syndrome; indicates a syndrome; rare syndrome; acquired immune deficiency syndrome (AIDS); premenstrual syndrome; Down/Down's syndrome; fetal alcohol syndrome

Exercises

H. **In each of the sentences below, the underlined collocation has an extra word in it. Cross out the extra word in the collocation. The first one is an example.**

1. Some American universities have been accused of <u>gender ~~toward~~ bias</u> because they give more sports scholarships to men than women.

2. When <u>the merger of</u> the Bank of the People <u>between and</u> the Public Trust Bank was announced, customers wondered what the new name would be.

3. Although he had just lost his job, he seemed to have a <u>positive distant outlook</u> on the future.

4. <u>Down disease syndrome</u> does not allow a child to develop normal physical and mental abilities.

5. Telling people that they look beautiful or handsome is one way to <u>flatter up their egos</u>.

6. After their defeat in the championship, the <u>morale</u> of the soccer team <u>was at rock solid bottom</u>.

7. <u>Failure not to disclose</u> all one's sources of income can get one in trouble with the tax officials.

8. Detectives often <u>reconstruct the actions events</u> leading up to a crime in order to improve their understanding of what happened.

9. The <u>wide disparity distance between</u> our salaries makes it impossible for us to pay equal amounts of the household expenses.

10. He listens to classical music when he grades his students' papers because he thinks it puts him in the <u>proper of mind-se</u>t for the job.

I. In each sentence, a phrase appears in boldface. For each boldface phrase, substitute a collocation from the collocations list. Write the collocation on the line. The first one is an example.

1. Although the professor was very knowledgeable in his field, his lack of **ability to interact with people** made it difficult for his students to discuss problems with him when they did not understand something from his lectures. <u>interpersonal skills</u>

2. Because of the recent political events, police officers were required to **look very closely at** the identity documents of people entering the building. _____

3. Although he had many skills to offer the company, he knew it would be hard to reach a managerial position because he was outside the **system in which old male friends favor each other.** _____

4. He was **deceiving himself** that he would be able to choose his own career, rather than do what his family expected of him. _____

5. Having academic arguments on challenging topics can help to **develop one's mind.** _____

6. The significant decrease in sales was a **really big change** from the sales predictions for the year. _____

7. The **increase in feelings** in support of the actor seemed to be in direct response to his terrible accident because his popularity was minimal before that.

_____

8. If I **continue to delay**, I will never get my work done! _____

Discussion or Writing

J. Answer the following questions.

1. Do you know any cures for temporary insomnia? What are they?

2. How is hypnosis viewed in your culture?

3. When you procrastinate, what do you usually do? Give an example.

4. How can one be sure not to alienate old friends when making new friends?

5. What do you consider to be a human being's primal characteristics?

Research

Word Form Chart

NOUN	VERB	ADJECTIVE	ADVERB
analysis	analyze	analytical	analytically
cause	cause	causal	causally
confirmation	confirm	confirmatory	
constraint	constrain	constraining	
control	control	controlled	
correlation	correlate	correlational	
criterion			
deduction	deduce	deductive	deductively
demonstration	demonstrate	demonstrative	
equivalence		equivalent	equivalently
equivalent			
experiment	experiment	experimental	experimentally
generalization	generalize		
hypothesis	hypothesize	hypothetical	hypothetically
induction	induce	inductive	inductively
manipulation	manipulate	manipulated	
observation	observe	observant	
		observed	
		observable	
prediction	predict	predictable	predictably
		predictive	
		predicted	
quality		qualitative	qualitatively
quantity		quantitative	quantitatively
randomness	randomize	random	randomly
reliability	rely	reliable	reliably
significance	signify	significant	significantly
subject			

NOUN	VERB	ADJECTIVE	ADVERB
validation	validate	valid validating validated	validly
validity variable	vary	variable varying	variably
variability variation			

Definitions and Examples

1. **analysis**, n. [the process of breaking something down into its component parts in order to understand it better; an oral or written report of findings obtained through this process]

   Doctors usually wait for a laboratory analysis of blood and urine before deciding on a lengthy course of treatment for a patient.

   Someone with an analytical learning style has an advantage in the study of grammar.

2. **cause**, v.t. [to bring about; to make something happen]

   A sudden change in temperature may cause people to become sick more easily.

   When two kinds of events tend to happen at about the same time, researchers look for a causal relationship between them.

3. **confirm**, v.t. [to add to evidence indicating that something is true or valid; to strengthen a feeling; to verify a hypothesis]

   The researcher found new data to confirm her hypothesis, so she submitted an article about her research to a scientific journal.

   Don't forget that a confirmation of your flight reservation is necessary the day before your departure.

4. constraint, n. [a limit, restriction or confinement; the condition of being limited, repressed, restricted, or confined]

> A university student collecting data for a thesis operates within certain constraints that protect his subjects' privacy.

> A creative researcher tries not to be constrained by currently accepted ideas when explaining unusual new data.

5. control, n. [a group of experimental subjects in which key variables are held constant, so that other groups may be compared with it; something which governs or limits action, emotion, or thinking]

> In any experiment, the control group must be carefully matched to the experimental group, so that they differ only in the characteristic that is being tested.

> Please control your child more carefully; she almost ran into the street.

6. correlation, n. [a consistent pattern of relationship between or among two or more things]

> In human beings, there is a positive statistical correlation between good nutrition in childhood and height in adulthood.

> Learning problems in children have been shown to correlate with recreational drug use by their parents, but whether the cause lies in biochemistry or in the emotional atmosphere of the home is not clear.

7. criterion, n. {pl. criteria} [a standard; a set value on the basis of which a decision or judgment is made]

> Professors usually explain in the syllabus the criteria by which they will measure students' success or failure in a course.

> When choosing a computer, most students consider price to be a major criterion.

8. deduction, n. [a logical reasoning process which uses general truths and logical principles to draw conclusions about specific cases; a fact that can be found by this process]

> The deductions of the police detective led to the quick arrest of a local teenager who had left his swim team jacket at the crime scene.

> Deductive reasoning works well only when one knows all the important facts.

9. **demonstration,** n. [an act which shows how something works or that something is true]

> The elementary school teacher set up a demonstration of how electricity works, using a circuit with a battery, a small lightbulb, and a switch.

> At the appliance store, a salesman demonstrated how to use the food processor.

10. **equivalent,** adj. [equal; comparable; the same in amount or importance]

> The two researchers got equivalent results when they conducted the same chemistry experiments on separate occasions and in separate laboratories.

> Students learning basic mathematics must learn to understand the concepts of addition, subtraction, and equivalence.

11. **experiment,** n. [a procedure in which certain characteristics are held constant and others are varied or manipulated, in order to test a hypothesis; an action whose result or outcome is uncertain]

> They experimented with different spices and oven temperatures, hoping to find the best recipe for roasted chicken.

> We were surprised by the outcome of the experiment, but we got the same results when we repeated it.

12. **generalization,** n. [a statement about a larger situation, type or group based only on information about specific examples; the thinking process that results in such a statement]

> Linguistic scholars work in a variety of languages, but they hope that their findings will enable them to discover generalizations about how people learn and use all languages.

> Is it fair to generalize and make judgments about an entire country if we have known only one or two of its citizens?

13. **hypothesis,** n. {pl. **hypotheses**}[a possible explanation for something, which can be tested by experiment or by observed data and either disproved or supported]

> Dr. Wolff's hypothesis about language teaching is that advanced students are not helped by being interrupted and corrected during a speaking class.

> Joseph said he was speaking about marriage only hypothetically, but I suspect he is making definite plans for his future.

14. **induction,** n. [a logical reasoning process which uses information about specific cases as the basis for making generalizations about larger groups of similar cases; the process of causing someone to do something]

> Inductive reasoning can be done successfully only on the basis of a large body of data.

> If I promise to pay for your ticket, can I induce you to go to the concert with me?

15. **manipulation,** n. [the handling or skillful changing of something for a specific purpose]

> It is acceptable research practice to manipulate experimental variables or conditions while testing a variety of hypotheses, but manipulating the data is completely unacceptable.

> Children can sometimes manipulate their parents in order to get what they want.

16. **observation,** n. [the process of watching or noticing something; a period of time during which this process takes place; what has been learned by watching or noticing something; a spoken or written communication about what has been learned through this process]

> A researcher must make careful observations or she will lose important data.

> I would like to observe your class on Thursday at 3:00 and then discuss it with you at a postobservation meeting.

17. **predict,** v.t. [to make a statement about what should be expected in the future, often based on data concerning past events]

> We predicted that our explanation of the experiment's results would be proven correct, but we were wrong.

> Some people think that certain natural signs, such as thickened fur on animals, are predictive of a cold winter.

18. **qualitative,** adj. [concerning the nature of things; characteristics that are describable but not countable]

> Social science reports often include more qualitative description than numerical data.

> Human behavior is often best analyzed qualitatively, at least until we are sure which characteristics or events are most important.

19. **quantitative,** adj. [concerning amount and number]

> A quantitative description of human interactions in a business meeting would include how many times a certain behavior, such as nods or handshakes, occurred.

> Physicists tend to see the world in quantitative terms, while an artist's view is likely to be more sensory and descriptive.

20. **random,** adj. [having a lack of order, purpose, plan, or method; unpredictable]

> Participants in the study were chosen by a random process and not to fit into any specific categories such as age, sex, or occupation.

> The randomness of the locations from which the cars had been stolen made the police suspect that several different groups of thieves were involved.

21. **reliability,** n. [the quality of trustworthiness, accuracy, or dependability; the probability that results will be consistent or that something will continue to function]

> The best thing about this old car is its reliability, even in cold weather.

> Good research is dependent on appropriate and reliable data collection methods.

22. **significance,** n. [importance; meaningfulness]

> The significance of the data cannot be determined until we know how much the results can vary just by chance.

> Identical twins generally have no significant differences in their appearance.

23. **subject,** n. [a person chosen to be part of an experiment, either in the control group or the experimental group]

> Every research institution requires its researchers to observe certain constraints that protect the privacy of experimental subjects.

> In a "double-blind" experiment, neither the subject nor the researcher knows whether or not the subject is in the control group.

24. **valid,** adj. [well based in fact; effective; appropriate; legally acceptable]

> Because the researcher's experimental design was faulty, several experts said his findings were not valid.

> The doctor's theory about the cause of the epidemic was validated by evidence collected after it was over.

25. **variable,** n. [a quality, property, or fact in an experiment; a situation that can be held constant or manipulated and that has a potential effect on the result]

> Variables that affect public health include immunization programs, clean water, prenatal care, regular health screening for schoolchildren, and adequate nutrition.

> Variability among human beings exists in appearance, abilities, and certain biochemical responses, but we are still more alike than we are different.

Exercises

A. Match each word with its definition or synonym.

___ 1. quantitative	a.	the same
___ 2. qualitative	b.	strengthen, support, verify
___ 3. criterion	c.	share patterned changes
___ 4. equivalent	d.	numerical
___ 5. observant	e.	figure something out
___ 6. confirm	f.	by chance
___ 7. generalize	g.	about what is describable
___ 8. reliable	h.	test or try something
___ 9. correlate	i.	factually correct
___ 10. manipulate	j.	standard or set value for decision making
___ 11. significance	k.	induce
___ 12. deduce	l.	seeing and noticing very well
___ 13. experiment	m.	make a sweeping statement from small bits of evidence
___ 14. predictable	n.	change something in a patterned way, for a reason
___ 15. cause	o.	expected; easily foreseen
___ 16. randomly	p.	trustworthy, dependable
___ 17. valid	q.	meaning

B. Answer each question with a word from the word form chart. Use the correct form of the word in your answer.

1. What is a possible explanation for something that has not been proved?

_____

2. What makes something happen? _____

3. What limits action or expression? _____

4. What is a pattern among data points? _____

5. How are we describing something when we use numbers for the description?

_____

6. What kind of logic requires us to collect lots of data about specific cases before drawing a conclusion? _____

7. What does a researcher want the experimental findings to do to her hypothesis?

_____

8. Who can be a source of experimental data? _____

9. How can we describe something without using numbers?

_____

C. Complete each analogy with a word from the word form chart.

1. forecast : result :: _____ : outcome

2. numerical : quantitative :: descriptive : _____

3. constant : variable :: patterned : _____

4. _____ : possible :: proven : real

5. _____ : experiment :: player : game

6. support : _____ :: prove : validate

7. _____ : valuable :: reliable : accurate

8. random : uncontrolled :: _____ : limitation

D. Write *T* if the sentence is true and *F* if it is false.

____ 1. Variables are changed for the control group during an experiment.

____ 2. If we see a correlation between two factors, we can be sure of a causal relationship.

____ 3. We can more easily predict the outcome of a scientific demonstration than of an experiment.

____ 4. Observation is the equivalent of experimentation.

____ 5. An experimental subject helps to design the experiment.

____ 6. Generalization and analysis are both thinking processes.

____ 7. Before choosing a computer, the customer should decide on the criteria that will help her to evaluate the various models.

____ 8. Inductive reasoning starts with specific examples to reach a generalization, whereas deductive reasoning reaches conclusions about specific cases by applying logic based on generalizations about groups.

____ 9. Significant research findings help us to understand our world.

____ 10. Random data correlate with each other.

____ 11. Scientists aim to control the design of an experiment so that unexpected variables do not affect the data.

E. Circle the correct answers. Some questions may have more than one correct answer.

1. Which are kinds of thinking?

    a. analysis   b. significance   c. criteria   d. deduction

2. Which are processes that reach conclusions by collecting specific data?

    a. deduction   b. generalization   c. reliability   d. induction

3. What do we call things that are alike in very important ways?

    a. analytical   b. valid   c. equivalent   d. hypothetical

4. Which are ways of getting information?

   a. observation   b. manipulation   c. experimentation   d. prediction

5. Which are desirable qualities for experimental results to have?

   a. validity   b. reliability   c. randomness   d. significance

6. What would a researcher like to have other researchers' work do to his or her findings?

   a. constrain   b. confirm   c. predict   d. validate

7. What qualities have to do with differences and lack of pattern?

   a. randomness   b. generalization   c. variability   d. prediction

8. Which are needed when one conducts an experiment?

   a. variation   b. demonstration   c. a control   d. analysis

9. How can we describe effective researchers?

   a. analytical   b. observant   c. manipulative   d. reliable

10. Quiet, shy people can be described in what way?

   a. controlled   b. constrained   c. predictive   d. variable

F. Read the three paragraphs. Then, in each blank, write the most appropriate word from the list given before each paragraph. The correct form of each word is given in the list. Some words may be used more than once.

Paragraph 1

significant   predictability   experiments   equivalent   criterion

        Although many people carelessly refer to scientific demonstrations and (1) _____ as if they were (2) _____ to each other, more than one (3) _____ difference exists between them. However, the most important (4) _____ by which we can distinguish them is the (5) _____ of the outcome.

Paragraph 2

predicted   demonstration   reliability   correlation   confirmed

        A scientific (6) _____ only shows a fact or a (7) _____ that has previously been observed and that has been (8) _____ by much previous experimentation. Therefore its outcome can be (9) _____ with great (10) _____. In a demonstration there is a well-understood causal relationship between one action or one variable and the predicted effect. Thus, a student can learn something new from observing a (11) _____, but an experienced researcher in that field of study will not.

Paragraph 3

validating   significant   experiment   experimental   variable

        In contrast, an (12) _____ can provide new information by (13) _____ a hypothesis or disproving it. When conducting experiments, scientists hope that the data will not be random and will lead to (14) _____ findings. In any case, (15) _____ results are potentially more (16) _____ and, therefore, less predictable than the results of a demonstration.

Collocations

1. **analysis**—the final analysis; statistical analysis; strategic analysis; data analysis; analytical talent; analytical frame of mind

2. **cause**—cause and effect; lost cause; probable cause; cause of death; causal relationship

3. **confirmation**—reservation confirmation; independent confirmation; written confirmation; official confirmation; awaiting confirmation

4. **constraint**—act as a constraint; built-in constraint; constraining factor

5. **control**—take control; lose control; remote control; control group; experimental control; beyond (one's) control; under control; arms control; birth control; gun control; disease control; traffic control

6. **correlation**—see a correlation; establish a correlation; close correlation; direct correlation

7. **criterion**—sole criterion; major criterion; criterion-referenced tests; criteria for success; criteria for selection

8. **deduction**—powers of deduction; deductive ability; make a deduction; logical deduction

9. **demonstration**—practical demonstration; mass demonstration; peaceful demonstration; violent demonstration; free demonstration

10. **equivalent**—roughly equivalent; closest equivalent; to an equivalent degree; equivalent to

11. **experiment**—laboratory experiment; perform an experiment; dangerous experiment; double-blind experiment; experimental subjects; scientific experiment; social experiment

12. **generalization**—broad generalization; faulty generalization; empirical generalization; exceptions to the generalization

13. **hypothesis**—test a hypothesis; plausible hypothesis; working hypothesis; support the hypothesis; hypothetical situation; hypothetical question; well-established hypothesis

14. **manipulation**—manipulate a variable; cynical manipulation; currency manipulation; media manipulation; dirty tricks and manipulation

15. **observation**—make an observation; interesting observation; accurate observation; observation platform; period of observation; careful observation; scientific observation

16. **prediction**—safe prediction; obvious prediction; weather prediction; unsettling prediction; accurate prediction; predictive validity; make a prediction

17. **qualitative**—qualitative change; qualitative difference; qualitative and quantitative; qualitative advantage; qualitative data; qualitative advance; qualitative research; qualitative description; qualitative approach

18. **quantitative**—quantitative analysis; quantitative research, quantitative description; quantitative approach

19. **randomness**—apparent randomness; sheer randomness; random chance; superficial randomness; random choice; random selection; at random

20. **reliability**—establish the reliability; improved reliability; overall reliability; complete reliability; test/retest reliability; quality and reliability; honesty and reliability; safety and reliability

21. **significance**—underscore the significance; statistical significance; full significance; special significance; question the significance; grasp the significance; strategic significance; no particular significance; significant glances

22. **validity**—predictive validity; of dubious validity; reliability and validity; scientific validation; establish the validity

23. **variable**—dependent variable; independent variable; highly variable; variable rate; manipulate a variable; degree of variability; normal variability; pattern of variability

Exercises

G. **In each sentence below, some words or phrases are underlined, and one or two words are in boldface. Circle the underlined words that frequently collocate with the word(s) in boldface. The first one is an example.**

1. Qualitative and quantitative research offer different kinds of <u>evidence</u>, but they may be <u>convincing</u> to a (roughly) **equivalent** (degree.)

2. In the <u>final</u> **analysis**, your <u>decision</u> must satisfy you and nobody else.

3. For a researcher, the best <u>outcome</u> would be to <u>publish</u> a discovery first, and then have <u>independent</u> **confirmation** through someone else's findings.

4. The **correlation** between depression and shortening hours of daylight was <u>established</u> long before the <u>cause</u> of the depression was found.

5. For a teenager <u>choosing</u> a car, the top speed may be the <u>sole</u> **criterion** for selection.

6. By examining the <u>generalization</u> on which it is based, we can sometimes <u>determine</u> whether a **deduction** is <u>logical</u>.

7. A researcher <u>conducting</u> a <u>double-blind</u> **experiment** does not <u>know</u> whether an **experimental** <u>subject</u> is in the control group.

8. A <u>well-established</u> **hypothesis** can be tested by <u>examining</u> its <u>predictive</u> **validity**.

9. After a <u>period</u> of **observation**, one can <u>collect</u> all the data and analyze it.

10. <u>Reliable weather</u> **prediction** can be achieved through an <u>analysis</u> of <u>correlations</u> in observed data.

11. The <u>full</u> **significance** of a new <u>hypothesis</u> may not be <u>grasped</u> for several years.

12. The application of new <u>technology</u> can give a <u>manufacturer</u> a **qualitative** <u>advantage</u> in making its products.

13. One can <u>manipulate</u> a **variable**, for example, by varying the <u>nutrition</u> given to <u>experimental</u> **subjects**, in order to look for <u>correlations</u> in the data.

H. In each sentence, part of a collocation appears in boldface. Complete each collocation and sentence by adding a word from the list of collocations. The first one is an example.

1. Medical researchers look for a **causal** <u>relationship</u> between a disease organism and an illness.

2. A theoretical explanation of how something works is often less informative than a(n) _____ **demonstration**.

3. A(n) _____ **generalization** can easily be reached when one does not have enough data on which to base a conclusion.

4. We should try not to worry about what is _____ **control**, since we are unable to affect the outcome.

5. **Criterion-**_____ _____ give very specific indications of what a learner understands and can do.

6. One _____ **constraint** on experimental scientific work is the money that is available to support the research.

7. It is necessary to _____ the **reliability** of a test before using the results to make important decisions.

8. **Quantitative** _____ is used in chemistry to help us to understand the composition of a substance.

9. A(n) _____ **prediction** is one that is suggested by all the available data.

Discussion or Writing

I. Answer the following questions.

1. Should governments, foundations, and companies give more money for theoretical research, which attempts to expand human knowledge, or for applied research, which is directed at solving a particular problem? Give reasons for your answer.

2. In what circumstances will qualitative research give more informative answers than quantitative research? In what circumstances will the opposite be true?

3. Should a researcher use data obtained from previous researchers, if the previous researchers abused their experimental subjects? Why or why not?

4. Is a researcher justified in falsifying data, if by so doing he or she can relieve human suffering? Give reasons for your answer.

Science

Word Form Chart

NOUN	VERB	ADJECTIVE	ADVERB
aroma		aromatic	aromatically
base		basic	
catalyst	catalyze	catalytic	
chain reaction			
chaos		chaotic	chaotically
cohesion	cohere	cohesive	cohesively
decomposition	decompose		
diffusion	diffuse	diffuse	diffusely
eclipse	eclipse		
elasticity		elastic	elastically
equation	equate	equal	equally
equilibrium			
evaporation	evaporate	evaporative	
fission		fissionable	
fusion	fuse		
inertia		inert	inertly
inhibitor	inhibit	inhibited	
ion	ionize	ionic	
lens			
molecule		molecular	
momentum			
nucleus		nuclear	
		organic	
prism		prismatic	
reflection	reflect	reflective	reflectively
solution	dissolve		
solvent			
spontaneity		spontaneous	spontaneously
volatility		volatile	

Definitions and Examples

1. **aromatic,** adj. [having a strong odor; chemically based on a ring of carbon atoms with a particular bond structure]

   Some aromatic substances are added to gasoline to improve its burning characteristics.

   Ginger and cinnamon are aromatic spices with distinct but pleasant aromas.

2. **base,** n. [the opposite of an acid; an alkali]

   Baking soda is a mild base that reacts with acid to form bubbles of gas.

   Weak bases tend to taste bitter; strong bases can damage tissues and should not be tasted or spilled on the skin.

3. **catalyst,** n. [a substance that is present in a chemical reaction and helps it to proceed or go faster, but that does not become part of the final product; a person or thing helping an interaction between or among people or organizations to proceed smoothly]

   Scientists frequently use catalysts to make experimental procedures happen more quickly.

   In a negotiation between two countries, a diplomat from a neutral third country may take part in order to act as a catalyst, helping the discussions to go smoothly and reach a successful conclusion.

4. **chain reaction,** n. [a process in which the products of a reaction help the process to continue; a continuing series of events, each causing or facilitating the next]

   Chemical chain reactions proceed slowly at first but speed up as more reaction products become available.

   In foggy or icy conditions, a two-car crash can become a chain reaction accident, as additional vehicles collide with the ones that have already stopped.

5. **chaos,** n. [a complete lack of organization]

   My desk is in a state of chaos; I cannot find anything.

   The meeting proceeded chaotically, since nobody knew who was supposed to give the reports.

6. **cohesion,** n. [the tendency of things to stay together as a unit]

In gases, forces promoting cohesion of molecules are not very strong.

To help achieve cohesion in your writing, use well-chosen transitional expressions between sentences and paragraphs.

7. **decomposition,** n. [the process by which a substance is transformed into simpler substances]

Digestion causes the decomposition of complex substances in foods to form simpler substances that the body can use.

The children showed the police the half-decomposed body that they had found in the woods near the playground.

8. **diffusion,** n. [the spreading of a substance within a space; the spreading of an idea within a social environment]

There is more diffusion of gas molecules at higher altitudes because of lower atmospheric pressure.

Diffusion of ideas and inventions from one culture to another is increased as communication becomes easier.

9. **eclipse,** n. [an event in which the shadow of the earth or the moon blocks out the light of the sun (solar eclipse) or in which the shadow of the earth blocks out the moon (lunar eclipse); the overshadowing of one person or event by another]

Hundreds of years ago, whenever there was a total solar eclipse, people feared that the world was ending.

The young chemist's amazing findings eclipsed the less exciting accomplishments of his colleagues.

10. **elasticity,** n. [the property that allows a substance to deform and then return to its original shape]

The elasticity of the plastic toy kept it from breaking when it was dropped on the tile floor.

Use an elastic band to hold that bunch of flowers together.

11. **equation,** n. [a statement of equality between two sets of mathematical terms; a statement of substances going into, and reaction products coming out of, a chemical reaction; a statement of equality between two elements]

Technical papers are often full of equations.

It is a mistake to equate wealth with happiness.

12. **equilibrium,** n. [a mental or physical stability; a situation in which forces or reactions in a system are balanced, such that the system tends not to change much over time]

> If precipitation and evaporation are about equal worldwide, then the Earth's water cycle is in equilibrium.

> He heard a buzzing in his ears, lost his equilibrium, and fell down the steps.

13. **evaporation,** n. [the process by which a liquid becomes a gas]

> If a sick person's skin is wiped with a damp cloth, evaporation will cause cooling and may reduce his fever.

> The thief disappeared into the crowd so quickly and silently that she seemed to evaporate into the air.

14. **fission,** n. [the division of something into two or more pieces; the process of splitting the nucleus, or center, of an atom to release tremendous amounts of energy]

> Fission is used to generate most atomic energy.

> Uranium is a fissionable material.

15. **fusion,** n. [a nuclear reaction in which the nuclei, or central parts, of atoms become one, generating much power; the merging of two objects into one]

> Fusion reactions are not used in power generation as often as fission reactions, despite the fact that they can produce more power.

> The empty frying pan and the metal element on the stove top became so hot that they melted and fused.

16. **inertia,** n. [the resistance of an object to changing from rest to motion or from motion to rest; any accumulation of custom or practice which makes social change difficult]

> It is hard to understand how an organism with such extreme inertia can be considered alive.

> There is so much inertia in this department that I do not think any changes will ever be made.

17. **inhibit,** v. [to reduce the likelihood that something will happen; to slow something down; to constrain emotional expression]

> It is possible to inhibit many chemical reactions by lowering the temperature.

> An inhibited person may feel extreme anger or joy but is unlikely to show them in her behavior.

18. **ion,** n. [an atom, part of an atom, or molecule with a positive or negative electrical charge]

    When a salt is in solution, it separates into ions.

    Ionizing radiation splits atoms or molecules into ions.

19. **lens,** n. [a piece of curved glass or plastic that affects the path of light, enlarging or reducing the perceived size of an object]

    The lenses in telescopes and microscopes have opposite effects.

    The eye doctor wrote me a prescription for contact lenses to correct my nearsightedness.

20. **molecule,** n. [the smallest unit of a substance that includes atoms of one, or more than one, element]

    Organic molecules contain carbon.

    Knowledge of molecular structure can help us to predict how one chemical will react with another.

21. **momentum,** n. [the property of an object that causes it to tend to keep moving in the manner and direction in which it is already moving]

    Student drivers must learn how far momentum will carry a car after braking.

    It's time to go home, but I'm afraid that if we stop working on the project now, we'll lose our momentum.

22. **nuclear,** adj. {n. sing. **nucleus;** pl. **nuclei**} [related to the center of atoms; related to the force or energy that can be generated by splitting or merging the centers of atoms]

    The explosion of a nuclear weapon creates huge, immediate damage and also long-term radiation damage to people's health.

    The nucleus of an atom is by far the heaviest part.

23. **organic,** adj. [containing carbon molecules; characteristic of living things or their products or residues]

    Organic molecules tend to be larger than most inorganic molecules.

    Organic gardening is done without pesticides or chemical fertilizers.

24. prism, n. [a crystal that splits visible white light into different colors]

The small crystals on her evening gown were like tiny prisms, sparkling in changing pastel colors.

Sunlight passed through the prism, and a rainbow of colored lights exited from the other side.

25. reflect, v. [to bounce back light or other radiation; to show that a character trait or a situation exists]

The baby stared at his reflection in the small mirror.

The architect's design for the new city hall reflected her concern and compassion for people with handicaps: she included sidewalk ramps and wide doors for wheelchairs.

26. solution, n. [a liquid that is mixed with a solid or gas, without any chemical reaction taking place]

When we open a carbonated soft drink, the carbon dioxide gas immediately begins to escape from the solution.

Sugar dissolves better in warm water than in cold.

27. solvent, n. [a substance that causes another to dissolve or disperse in a liquid]

Solvents are often used to remove something that is stuck on a surface or in a container.

Organic solvents frequently have distinctive odors.

28. spontaneous, adj. [occurring without previous plan or obvious cause]

A spontaneous reaction occurred when sunlight coming through the window heated the liquid in the beaker.

The party developed spontaneously when the five classmates discovered that they had no plans for that night.

29. volatile, adj. [changing easily into a gas; tending to change easily or to become angry easily]

Solid carbon dioxide, known as "dry ice," is extremely volatile at room temperature.

Patricia lost her job working with children because of her emotional volatility.

Exercises

A. Circle the correct answers. Some questions will have more than one correct answer.

1. Which affect(s) the speed of a reaction?

   a. catalyst   b. aroma   c. ion   d. inhibitor

2. Which can describe how compact a substance is?

   a. lens   b. spontaneous   c. diffuse   d. cohesive

3. Which refer(s) to the formation of gases?

   a. reflection   b. volatility   c. evaporation   d. momentum

4. Which describe(s) molecular structure or composition?

   a. organic   b. aromatic   c. reflective   d. inhibited

5. Which are processes that generate huge amounts of energy?

   a. elasticity   b. equilibrium   c. fission   d. fusion

6. Which refer(s) to states of rest or motion?

   a. reflection   b. momentum   c. solvent   d. inertia

7. Which can focus or split light?

   a. lens   b. prism   c. evaporation   d. catalyst

8. Which name(s) the center of an atom?

   a. inhibitor   b. molecule   c. nucleus   d. base

9. Which refer(s) to a continuing process?

   a. spontaneity   b. inertia   c. aroma   d. chain reaction

10. Which involve(s) something hiding something else?

    a. inertia   b. lens   c. eclipse   d. catalyst

B. Complete each analogy with a word or phrase from the word form chart.

1. _____ : rigid :: spontaneous : programmed

2. unpredictable : reliable :: _____ : calm

3. sour : bitter :: acid : _____

4. equilibrium : balance :: _____ : disorder

5. ascend : climb :: _____ : rot

6. small : _____ :: large : galaxy

7. _____ : symbols :: sentence : words

8. mirror : _____ :: prism : rainbow

9. hide : _____ :: show : reveal

10. ice : melt :: liquid : _____

11. inert : _____ :: cohesive : diffuse

C. Circle the word or phrase that is least related in meaning to the others.

1. spontaneous	planned	programmed
2. fission	fusion	equilibrium
3. diffuse	dissolved	ionic
4. prism	nucleus	lens
5. acid	base	solvent
6. aromatic	fissionable	nuclear
7. momentum	chain reaction	lens
8. chain reaction	aroma	odor
9. cohesion	catalyst	diffusion
10. diffusion	combining	fusion
11. balance	chaos	confusion
12. evaporate	melt	equate
13. decomposition	breaking apart	inertia

14. reflection   solution   light

15. disorder   chaos   equilibrium

16. inhibit   diffuse   slow

D. Write *T* if the sentence is true and *F* if it is false.

____ 1. A solvent causes something to diffuse into a liquid.

____ 2. A solution is composed of more than one substance.

____ 3. Inhibited people like to tell jokes at noisy parties.

____ 4. Nuclear fusion is used as a power source for automobiles.

____ 5. Acid is strongly basic.

____ 6. A chain reaction auto accident involves only two vehicles.

____ 7. To reduce chaos in your room, you can sort your books and papers so that everything needed for each course is in the same place.

____ 8. Heat applied to a liquid will cause evaporation to take place.

____ 9. Water droplets in the air can act as prisms, producing a rainbow.

____ 10. A reflective surface causes light to be absorbed.

____ 11. The momentum of a rocket allows it to continue on its way without the constant use of more fuel.

____ 12. For the best human environment, we need to keep industrial development and environmental protection in equilibrium.

E. Match each word or phrase with its definition or synonym.

____ 1. chain reaction   a. cause light to bounce back

____ 2. volatile   b. a molecule with a charge

____ 3. basic   c. staying together

____ 4. elasticity   d. what splits light into colors

____ 5. spontaneous   e. what causes a solid to disperse in a liquid

___ 6. solvent

f.   the ability to bend and resume a former shape

___ 7. prism

g.   a process in which one reaction causes the next one

___ 8. ion

h.   what can make an image seem larger or smaller

___ 9. cohesive

i.   unplanned

___ 10. lens

j.   easily becoming gaseous

___ 11. reflect

k.   not acid

F. Read the passage. Then, in each blank, write the most appropriate word from the choices in parentheses.

(1) _____ (prismatic, nuclear, inert) reactions, which involve the centers of atoms, are of two types: (2) _____ (fission, reflection, equilibrium) and (3) _____ (momentum, evaporation, fusion). Fission, which is a sort of (4) _____ (decomposition, solution, inhibitor) of the atom, disrupts the (5) _____ (spontaneous, cohesive, elastic) forces that normally hold the atom together. It results in more dangerous waste products than does (6) _____ (volatility, evaporation, fusion). Thus, when using fission in a nuclear power station, it is very important to be ready to (7) _____ (equate, catalyze, inhibit) a reaction that might go out of control even though it is highly unlikely that, in a well-designed and properly operated power station, a (8) _____ (molecular, volatile, nuclear) reaction will begin (9) _____ (aromatically, spontaneously, reflectively). Good engineering and well-trained personnel will help to prevent the (10) _____ (aroma, equation, chaos) and injury that would follow a serious nuclear accident.

G. Complete the crossword puzzle using words from the word form chart. One answer has been given.

Across

2. It splits light.
5. not planned
7. a state of balance
12. of the smallest unit of a substance
14. about something that changes the rate of a reaction
16. a preposition (given)
19. about the middle of an atom
20. not moving or reacting
21. It bends light.
23. a statement of equality or process
25. a state of disorganization
26. molecules with charge
27. with *reaction*, describes a process that tends to continue

Down

1. spread out; thin
3. slow down; prevent
4. It keeps things going.
6. It disperses a solid in a liquid.
7. to change from liquid to gas
8. containing a ring of carbon
9. light, bounced back
10. solid or gas, mixed in liquid
11. to reduce to a simpler form
13. easily becoming a gas
15. to stick together
17. a nuclear process
18. bendable
22. splitting atoms
24. not at all acidic

Collocations

1. **aroma**—aromatic compound; aromatic herbs; aromatic spirits of ammonia; enticing aroma; pleasant aroma

2. **base**—acid or base; basic reagents

3. **catalyst**—catalytic converter; catalytic process; chemical catalyst; social catalyst; serve as a catalyst; act as a catalyst; a catalyst of change

4. **chain reaction**—nuclear chain reaction

5. **chaos**—total chaos; descend into chaos; deteriorate into chaos; chaotic situation

6. **cohesion**—cohesive force; lack of cohesion

7. **decomposition**—thermal decomposition; decomposed corpse

8. **diffusion**—gaseous diffusion; cultural diffusion

9. **elasticity**—elastic band; coefficient of elasticity; elasticity of demand

10. **equation**—chemical equation; integral equation; differential equation

11. **equilibrium**—state of equilibrium; dynamic equilibrium; static equilibrium; emotional equilibrium; maintain equilibrium

12. **evaporation**—slow evaporation; rapid evaporation; evaporative cooling; evaporation loss control device

13. **fission**—nuclear fission; fission reactor; fission products

14. **fusion**—nuclear fusion; fusion reactor

15. **inertia**—inert gases; moment of inertia; inertia and momentum; overcome inertia

16. **inhibitor**—inhibit growth; inhibit development; inhibited personality; inhibit a process; feel inhibited

17. **ion**—ion exchange; ionizing radiation

18. **lens**—contact lens; grind a lens; camera lens

19. **molecule**—molecular weight; molecular structure; at the molecular level

20. **momentum**—gain momentum; lose momentum; maintain momentum; momentum and inertia

21. **nucleus**—nuclear reactor; nuclear energy; nuclear chain reaction; atomic nucleus

22. **organic**—organic molecules; organic solvent; organic compound; organic gardening; organically grown

23. **reflection**—reflect light; clear reflection; reflective material; reflective coating; reflective surface

24. **solution**—dilute solution; concentrated solution; neutral solution; acidic solution; basic solution

25. **solvent**—organic solvent; strong solvent

26. **spontaneous**—spontaneous reaction; spontaneous combustion

27. **volatility**—volatile liquid; volatile personality

Exercises

H. In each blank, write the appropriate collocation from the list at the beginning of each paragraph. You may use a collocation more than once. The first one is an example.

Paragraph 1

cohesive force   dilute solution   gaseous diffusion   strong solvent

If a (1) _strong solvent_ dissolves a small amount of a solid substance into a large amount of liquid, a (2)_____ is produced. The original solid substance has very little (3) _____ holding it together, since its molecules have diffused among those of the liquid. In fact, liquids and especially gases are not very cohesive at all. One indication of this is how (4)_____ allows the molecules of one gas to disperse among the molecules of another gas, or to spread widely in a vacuum.

Paragraph 2

catalytic converters   evaporative cooling   organic solvents

reflective coatings   contact lenses   volatile liquid   emotional equilibrium

Most of us are not fully aware of how much and how automatically we use the results of scientific exploration and discovery in our daily lives. For example, (5)_____ help to correct our faulty vision. Our cars have (6)_____ near the tailpipes, to reduce air pollution. We use (7)_____, such as carbon tetrachloride, to dry-clean our clothes. Someone who has significant depression may take a medication in order to maintain a reasonable (8)_____ and be able to function well in society. When someone is ill, we may sponge the person with alcohol, which is a (9)_____ that evaporates quickly and causes the (10)_____ that helps to reduce a high fever. Finally, we often add (11)_____ to everyday objects, such as machinery, clothing, and buildings, in order to prevent heat buildup and to make them easier to see.

Paragraph 3

atomic nuclei   fission products   fission reactor   nuclear fusion

nuclear energy   nuclear chain reaction

(12)_____ takes place inside our sun and other stars and generates much (13)_____. Because this reaction is self-sustaining, we say that it is a (14)_____. On Earth, (15)_____ is produced in a (16)_____, in which the (17)_____ are split. Although this process is obviously more controlled than the fusion which occurs on such a massive scale inside a star, one significant problem remains: (18)_____ resulting from the reaction are radioactive and must be disposed of very carefully.

I. Complete each collocation with one of the choices given below each sentence. The first one is an example.

1. When the prime minister was assassinated, we were afraid the army would take control of the government, because the political situation had **deteriorated into** _chaos_ .

   a. a state of equilibrium   b. chaos   c. a nuclear chain reaction

2. Our guests brought a bunch of spring flowers wrapped in white paper and held together with an **elastic** _____.

   a. band   b. coefficient   c. demand

3. When we study how solid objects behave in the presence of forces, we learn about **momentum and** _____.

   a. inertia   b. seconds   c. importance

4. The _____ **equation** told us what to expect when we added a certain substance to the solution.

   a. integral   b. chemical   c. differential

5. The strong-smelling organic **compound** was _____.

   a. chaotic   b. prismatic   c. aromatic

6. **Ionizing** _____ is a form of energy that causes molecules in the upper atmosphere to take on an electric charge.

   a. molecules   b. radiation   c. exchange

7. When heat is added and simpler compounds are produced from more complex ones, the process is called **thermal** _____.

   a. decomposition   b. volatility   c. aroma

J. Circle the underlined word or words that collocate with the word in boldface. The first one is an example.

1. The (liquid) has a high **volatility**, so the shipper must use a well-sealed container.

2. The firefighters blamed **spontaneous** combustion for the unexpected fire.

3. We need a strong organic **solvent** to remove the sticky tar from the body of the truck.

4. The dilute **solution** of baking soda in water was not strongly **basic**.

5. **Organic** compounds are often aromatic.

6. When we walk at night we should wear light-colored clothing or clothing made of material that **reflects** light, so that drivers can see us.

7. The chemists conducted a series of experiments to determine the **molecular** structure of the unknown substance.

8. The glassmaker had to grind the **lens** to exact specifications.

Discussion or Writing

K. Answer the following questions.

1. What recent discovery in physics or chemistry has had the most influence on your life?

2. It is said that technology and scientific concepts that we do not understand are impossible to distinguish from magic. What advantages, if any, are there for a country in having a scientifically literate population? How do you think a government could best educated its citizens for scientific literacy?

Society

Word Form Chart

NOUN	VERB	ADJECTIVE	ADVERB
assimilation	assimilate		
bigot		bigoted	
bigotry			
conformist	conform	conformist	
conformity			
dialogue			
domain			
double standard			
empowerment	empower	empowering	
		empowered	
gender			
heterogeneity		heterogeneous	
hierarchy		hierarchical	hierarchically
homogeneous	homogenize	homogeneous	
		indigenous	
latency		latent	
mobility	mobilize	mobile	
prestige		prestigious	
principles			
recluse		reclusive	
status quo			
stereotype	stereotype	stereotypical	stereotypically
suppression	suppress	suppressed	
		veritable	veritably
withdrawal	withdraw	withdrawn	

Definitions and Examples

1. **assimilate,** v.t. [to become like members of a group; to become a member of the group]

   Many immigrants want to assimilate into their new culture as quickly as possible.

   The assimilation of new populations into a community can create a unique combination of cultures in a small geographical area.

2. **bigotry,** n. [an intolerance of opinions, beliefs, races, or religions different from one's own]

   Organizations that support human rights consistently fight against bigotry.

   When making speeches, politicians usually avoid bigoted language so that they do not offend any voters.

3. **conform,** v.i. [to act in a way similar to a larger group; to follow a custom]

   A teenager usually conforms to the clothing styles of his schoolmates.

   New artists often fight against conformity to the mainstream so that their work will stand apart from the work of others.

4. **dialogue,** n. [a conversation or discussion between two or more people]

   The two groups that had opposed each other started a dialogue in order to find points of agreement.

   The audience could not hear the dialogue of the actors because the stage microphones were not working.

5. **domain,** n. [an area under particular control or influence; an area of knowledge]

   During the conflict among rival nations, citizens were encouraged not to travel beyond the domain of their home country.

   The attorney could not answer the client's question because it demanded knowledge outside his domain.

6. **double standard,** n. [a rule or custom that unfairly treats one group more severely than another under the same circumstances]

   The school demonstrated many instances of double standards of punishment, for example, punishing girls but not boys for fighting.

   In any society, double standards might fall along gender, education, or income lines.

7. **empower,** v.t. [to give a person or group power, authority, or confidence]

Reading empowers people because it gives them access to knowledge.

The right to vote empowered women to influence political decisions that would directly affect them.

8. **gender,** n. [the classification of living things as female or male]

In some countries, it is against the law to deny a person a job because of gender, age, race, or sexual orientation.

Although a person may physically be one sex, he or she might identify with the other gender.

9. **heterogeneous,** adj. [having very different characteristics or qualities within a group]

The people of the United States are a very culturally heterogeneous population.

The teacher had to design a variety of tasks for each lesson because of the heterogeneity of the class.

10. **hierarchy,** n. [a system in which individuals have different ranks]

In the hierarchy of public school personnel, the superintendent of schools has the highest rank, followed by the principals, vice-principals, department chairs, teachers, and finally staff.

The organizations of most governments follow a hierarchical system.

11. **homogeneous,** adj. [having very similar characteristics or qualities within a group]

Throughout world history, some people in power have tried to make their societies more homogeneous by killing members of targeted cultural groups.

All the members of the organization wore the same uniform, which gave them an appearance of homogeneity.

12. **indigenous,** adj. [originally from a particular place]

In the 2000 Olympics, an athlete representing the indigenous people of Australia lit the flame in the opening ceremony.

One way to avoid having to irrigate gardens in a very dry area is to use plants that are indigenous to that place and do not need much water.

13. latent, adj. [present but not openly or visibly; existing but not fully developed or active]

> The latent tension between the two communities became open hostility when one leader publicly called the other group enemies.

> There is a latency period in the initial development of cancer and some other diseases during which the illness cannot be detected.

14. mobile, adj. [able to move or be moved]

> Many automobile accidents are caused when people pay more attention to their mobile phones than to their driving.

> In today's computer job market, mobility of personnel is not as big an issue as it once was because people are able to use the Internet to work from their homes rather than from an office at a company location.

15. prestige, n. [an excellent reputation, usually because of achievement or success]

> Private colleges in the United States often have greater prestige than state-funded colleges.

> Working for a prestigious law firm helped Kevin meet the most influential people in the city.

16. principles, n. [a set of beliefs about right and wrong; personal ethics]

> When Dan suggested that we steal a copy of the test, I told him that he did not have any principles.

> He was a highly respected police chief because the public thought he was a principled man.

17. reclusive, adj. [secluded; private; avoiding people]

> Many senior citizens led reclusive lives before the introduction of the Internet into their homes. Now, they can communicate with a variety of people all over the world.

> If a millionaire becomes a recluse, it may be due to a fear of people trying to get his money all the time.

18. status quo (Latin), n. [the current condition or situation]

The members of a society who enjoy the most privileges usually want to maintain the status quo.

Social reformers want to change the status quo.

19. stereotype, n. [an unfair and simplified image of a person or people]

Children learn cultural stereotypes from their parents and from the media, but they often change their thinking when they actually interact with people who are different from them.

Hockey fans are frequently stereotyped as male, loud, and rude, but in fact they can be men or women who are quietly focused on the game and very polite.

20. suppression, n. [the act of stopping or preventing, sometimes by force]

The suppression of basic human rights often has led to revolution.

Some members of the government tried to suppress the damaging information, but a newspaper report soon made it public.

21. veritable, adj. [true] {usually used to emphasize a characteristic of something by means of a comparison}

The bird sanctuary that we visited in North Carolina is a veritable playground for anything that flies.

Garage sales can be veritable gold mines because one person's trash is another person's treasure.

22. (a) withdraw, v.i. [to move oneself away from or out of a group, physically, socially, or emotionally]

Because Martha had been such a sociable girl, her teacher realized something must be wrong when she withdrew from her friends at school and played by herself.

(b) withdraw, v.t. [to remove or take away]

If you want to withdraw money from your bank account, be sure to take photo identification with you and record the withdrawal in your account book.

Exercises

A. Match each word with its definition or synonym.

___ 1.	withdraw	a.	act in a similar way
___ 2.	reclusive	b.	excellent reputation
___ 3.	assimilate	c.	present but not yet visible
___ 4.	suppress	d.	native to a place
___ 5.	homogeneous	e.	area of control or knowledge
___ 6.	latent	f.	similar
___ 7.	bigotry	g.	become part of a group
___ 8.	prestige	h.	private
___ 9.	conform	i.	move away from a group
___ 10.	mobile	j.	prevent or keep something down
___ 11.	indigenous	k.	able to move
___ 12.	domain	l.	intolerance

B. Answer each question with a word or phrase from the word form chart. Use the correct form of the word or phrase in your answer.

1. How can one describe someone who is intolerant of another's religious beliefs?

   _____

2. What do you call the conversation between actors on a stage?

   _____

3. If a system of grading papers favors female students over male students, what does it reflect? _____

4. How would you describe a group where everyone is from a different country and is a different age?_____

5. What does one call a system where people have different ranks, some higher and some lower?_____

6. If people do not want change, what do they prefer? _____

7. How do people describe a university that has an excellent reputation?

_____

C. Write *T* if the sentence is true and *F* if it is false.

___ 1. A stereotype of a particular group is usually developed by people who have a great deal of experience working with individuals in that group.

___ 2. A veritable disaster should not be considered a problem.

___ 3. The leader of a medical research institution should be a principled individual.

___ 4. Inclusion in a company's decision-making process contributes to employee empowerment.

___ 5. Dividing a group by gender would lead to groups consisting of people of the same age.

___ 6. If a geographical domain is claimed by two countries, mapmakers may be unsure of how to identify the area.

___ 7. Opening a dialogue with someone you do not like is usually an easy task.

___ 8. A recluse is sure to attend every party to which he is invited.

___ 9. In a business hierarchy, an employee ranks higher than a manager does.

___ 10. A person who is indigenous to an area will normally know more about the area than someone who recently moved there.

D. Match each word with its opposite.

___ 1. homogeneous   a. encourage

___ 2. withdraw   b. weaken

___ 3. suppress   c. obvious

___ 4. empower   d. foreign

___ 5. mobile   e. sociable

___ 6. indigenous   f. tolerant

___ 7. latent   g. heterogeneous

___ 8. reclusive   h. separate

___ 9. bigoted   i. deposit

___ 10. assimilate   j. stationary

E. Write a word or phrase from the word form chart that restates or is a synonym of each boldface word or phrase.

1. Every time I try to set up a **discussion** with him, he tells me that he is too busy.

   _____

2. The queen realized that because of her illness, she would soon not be able to rule her **realm.** _____

3. The company must stop using **a strict system** to evaluate union employees **and an easy system** to evaluate nonunion employees.

   _____

4. Angela wanted to behave differently from her classmates, but the peer pressure was too strong, and she finally **acted like the majority.**

   _____

5. Schools of different kinds are established by society to cultivate the **undeveloped and still hidden** abilities of students with various talents.

   _____

6. When we had finished listing all the movies we wanted to see during our vacation, we realized we had created a **true** film festival for ourselves.

   _____

7. The student had always dreamed of attending a **highly thought of** university.

   _____

8. Many of our conflicts arose because we had different **personal ethical values.**

   _____

F. Read the passage. Then, in each blank, write an appropriate word or phrase from the list below. Use the correct form of each word.

status quo	stereotype	gender	veritable
suppress	empower	dialogue	mobile
hierarchy	domain	conform	bigot

Watching an international sporting event like the Olympics on American television gives one insights into different aspects of the society. In particular, one can understand how athletes are not only great in their own (1)_____ but also a strong influence in American society. For example, the issue of athletes as salespeople can be understood by watching advertisements on TV. In the United States, one minute people can watch a track and field event with a famous American athlete, and the next minute they can watch the same athlete in a commercial for a (2)_____ phone service.

A second example also indicates the importance of premier athletes in our society. A great amount of media coverage is given to the athletes, who are expected to bring home medals. After each event, the number of reporters, cameras, and microphones around the star seems a (3)_____ media circus. Later, the pictures, interviews, and stories are on the news and in the papers.

A third issue is how American society views athletes after they retire from their sports. Although these athletes are no longer on the field, many are now on the air as sports announcers. During the Olympics, radio listeners will hear (4)_____ between these former athletes and regular sports announcers. A few listeners have complained that there is too much of this and have asked for change, but having former athletes conduct interviews and provide commentary seems to be so popular that the (5)_____ is sure to be maintained by every network.

Last, the place of the athlete in America's social (6) _____ can be noted. The media spend many weeks and millions of dollars covering the Olympic games. Never is the same amount of money spent in showing outstanding teachers, wonderful parents, or effective nurses. In sum, when we watch the Olympics, we see what some have called America's royalty: athletes!

Collocations

1. **assimilate**—assimilate into the community; assimilate to a way of life; assimilate to a culture; cultural assimilation

2. **bigotry**—bigotry or prejudice; blatant bigotry; display bigotry; bigotry against; racial bigotry

3. **conform**—conform to a group; conformity to a stereotype; conform to specifications

4. **dialogue**—have a dialogue with someone; open a dialogue with someone; dialogue between X and Y; continuing dialogue

5. **domain**—different domains; public domain; private domain

6. **double standard**—have a double standard; apply a double standard; be subject to a double standard; victim of a double standard

7. **empower**—empower somebody to do something; empower people; empower women

8. **gender**—gender roles; gender bias

9. **heterogeneous**—heterogeneous group(s); heterogeneous population; heterogeneous society

10. **hierarchy**—rise in the hierarchy; social hierarchy; in the hierarchy; hierarchical organization

11. **homogeneous**—homogeneous group(s); homogeneous population(s); homogeneous societies

12. **indigenous**—indigenous population; indigenous peoples; indigenous to an area

13. **latent**—latent energy; latent talent; latent ability; latent potential; latent power; latent feelings; latent conflict; latent hostility; latent tension

14. **mobile**—upwardly mobile; mobile phone; mobile home

15. **prestige**—have prestige; gain prestige; great prestige; high prestige; low prestige; little prestige

16. **principles**—basic principles; adhere to one's principles; have principles

17. **reclusive**—aging recluse; reclusive way of life

18. **status quo**—maintain the status quo; support the status quo; restore the status quo; upset the status quo

19. **stereotype**—conform to a stereotype; negative stereotype; perpetuate a stereotype; stereotype people; stereotypical behavior

20. **suppression**—suppression of protests; suppression of dissent; violent suppression; suppress evidence; suppress a cough; suppress a smile

21. **veritable**—veritable paradise; veritable treasure; veritable feast

22. **withdraw**—withdraw money from a bank; withdraw support from; withdraw troops; forced to withdraw; strategic withdrawal

Exercises

G. **In each sentence, part of a collocation is underlined and part of it is missing. Complete each sentence by writing the missing part of the collocation in the blank. The first one is an example.**

1. Women as caretakers and men as income earners are examples of _gender roles_ in many societies.

2. Although her father treated her and her brother differently, she never felt that he _____ a double standard of behavior.

3. Before vacations, people often _____ money from a bank and buy travelers' checks so that if they lose the checks, they won't really lose their money.

4. Usually a student's _____ abilities can be developed by the right type of education.

5. Racial _____ is a continuing problem in many countries.

6. The workers and the management hope that the continuing _____ between the union and company leaders results in an end to the strike.

7. One can gain _____ just by spending time with people of higher status.

8. When immigrants arrive in a new country, they often <u>assimilate into the new</u> _____ and yet still maintain many aspects of their cultural heritage.

9. Based on her desire to succeed and her abilities, I would describe her as _____ <u>mobile</u>.

10. Showing a limited number of pictures when representing a group, especially pictures that do not show the diversity within the group, can help to <u>perpetuate a</u> _____ of that group.

H. Complete each sentence by circling the letter of the word or phrase that frequently collocates with the word in boldface. The first one is an example.

1. If we cannot _____ to our own **principles,** we cannot expect others to do the same.

   a. listen   (b.) adhere

2. We rejected the product because it did not **conform** to _____.

   a. specifications   b. dimensions

3. No matter if one lives in a **heterogeneous** or a **homogeneous** _____, one will find individuals with different interests and abilities.

   a. society   b. area

4. Chefs often try to include on their menus foods made with ingredients that are **indigenous** _____ because these items are fresher than ones shipped in from afar.

   a. to a town   b. to an area

5. Although her Ph.D. is in education, she enjoys working in many _____ **domains**.

   a. different   b. well-paying

6. The defense attorney tried **to suppress** _____.

   a. the judge   b. the evidence

7. The school administrators wanted to _____ **the status quo** regarding students attending their meetings because they wanted to limit the information shared with students.

   a. maintain   b. develop

8. In order to _____ in the **hierarchy** of the business, he took additional business classes.

   a. succeed   b. rise

9. The food at the conference reception was a **veritable** _____.

   a. dinner   b. feast

10. Several poets, like Emily Dickinson, were said to lead **reclusive** _____.

   a. lives   b. careers

Discussion or Writing

I. Answer the following questions.

1. Do you think that one should conform to the norms of one's culture? Why or why not?

2. What are some examples of double standards for men and women in your culture?

3. What should be done if a company tries to suppress information about a product that is dangerous?

4. How can teachers empower students to succeed in life?

5. Do you know about indigenous peoples in any country? Do they face any problems of bigotry or discrimination? Explain.

Answer Key

Unit 1

A. 1. d   2. j   3. g   4. e   5. a   6. m   7. h   8. b   9. k   10. i
11. f   12. c   13. l

B. 1. (the) acoustics   2. pristine   3. inevitable   4. donation   5. venue
6. (the) media   7. perceptive   8. seminal   9. depicting   10. lyrics

C. 1. F   2. F   3. T   4. T   5. T   6. F   7. T   8. T   9. F   10. F

D. 1. vicarious   2. truth   3. recently   4. upheaval   5. sell   6. disapprove
7. pleasure   8. donate   9. antique   10. trivial

E. 1. venue   2. semblance   3. origin   4. exhibitor   5. functioning
6. acoustic   7. endorse   8. obsessed

F. Answers will vary.

G. 1. change of   2. work   3. be on   4. generous   5. process   6. establish a
7. along a   8. live   9. unknown   10. properly   11. product   12. depth
13. poetry

H. 1. some semblance of order   2. major upheaval   3. trials and tribulations
4. in pristine condition   5. obsessed with money   6. approve . . . funding
7. acoustic instruments   8. contemporary look   9. inevitable result
10. accurate depiction   11. along a continuum   12. compose the lyrics

I. Answers will vary.

Unit 2

A. 1. j 2. e 3. h 4. i 5. k 6. l 7. f 8. b 9. c 10. a
11. d 12. g

B. 1. wholesaler 2. vendor (marketer, retailer, wholesaler) 3. potential
4. recession 5. retailer 6. sector 7. retaining 8. trader 9. trademark

C. 1. F 2. T 3. F 4. T 5. T 6. F 7. T 8. F 9. F
10. F 11. T 12. F 13. F

D. 1. recession 2. merger 3. innovate 4. principal 5. exploitation
6. secret 7. trade 8. client 9. invitation 10. vendor

E. 1. client 2. sector 3. innovation 4. trademark 5. discount
6. brainstorming 7. entrepreneur 8. negotiate

F. 1. recession 2. sectors 3. wholesale 4. brainstorming 5. vending
6. trademark 7. allocate 8. sector 9. discount 10. retailers
11. merge 12. potential 13. exploit 14. negotiating 15. retaining
16. patent 17. discreet

G. 1. resources, fairly 2. ideas, plans 3. help, serve 4. witness, evidence
5. store, rate 6. exercise, absolute 7. successful, business 8. resources,
commercial 9. idea, concept 10. stock, open 11. proposal, with
12. under, process 13. pending, apply for 14. benefit, fulfill

H. (a) 1. to each 2. severe 3. price 4. control 5. private
6. international 7. famous 8. licensed 9. merchant

(b) Answers will vary.

I. Answers will vary.

Unit 3

A. 1. d 2. g 3. h 4. i 5. b 6. c 7. a 8. j 9. f 10. e.

B. 1. transmit 2. enlighten 3. digress 4. discrepancy 5. perception
6. interface 7. verbal 8. semantics 9. rhetoric 10. pun

C. 1. amplification 2. cellular 3. feedback 4. metaphor
5. elaborate *or* amplify 6. improvise 7. pun 8. intentional
9. interface 10. confidential

D. 1. F   2. F   3. T   4. T   5. F   6. F   7. F   8. T   9. F

E. 1. confidential   2. melodramatic   3. perception   4. systematic
   5. adaptable   6. constructive   7. digress   8. enlighten

F. 1. understate   2. enlighten   3. improvised   4. cynical   5. systematic
   6. feedback   7. transmit   8. verbal or rhetorical   9. pun   10. metaphor

G. 1. understatement   2. improvised   3. confidential   4. constructive
   5. systematically   6. rhetorical   7. puns   8. semantics   9. monologue
   10. melodramatic   11. digress   12. verbal   13. cynical   14. enlighten
   15. feedback   16. perception

H. (a) 1. criticism   2. as best you can   3. obvious   4. action   5. educate
   6. skills   7. lengthy   8. strict   9. network   10. performance
   11. clearly   12. further

   (b) Answers will vary.

I. 1. highly adaptable   2. major discrepancy   3. get feedback
   4. systematic approach   5. perfect metaphor   6. reinforce the perception
   7. openly cynical   8. brief digression   9. fiery rhetoric   10. transmit data
   11. question of semantics   12. something of an understatement

J. Answers will vary.

Unit 4

A. 1. c   2. f   3. d   4. a   5. h   6. b   7. e   8. g   9. j   10. i

B. 1. F   2. T   3. F   4. T   5. F   6. T   7. T   8. F

C. 1. a, d   2. b, c   3. a, c   4. a, d   5. c, d

D. 1. back up   2. network   3. upgrade   4. icon   5. default   6. browser
   7. install   8. crashed   9. log on   10. glitch

E. 1. applications *or* programs *or* software   2. software *or* applications *or* programs
   3. cursor   4. scroll   5. icons   6. default   7. compatible   8. crashed
   9. back up   10. backup   11. search engines   12. browser   13. installed
   14. encrypt   15. download   16. home page   17. glitch   18. virus
   19. upgrade   20. hard drive

F. **Across** 1. back up   5. icon   6. glitch   8. download   11. programmer
14. crash   16. install   18. output   19. cursor   20. encrypt   21. virus

Down 1. browser   2. upgrade   3. network   4. scroll   7. application
9. default   10. compatible   12. software   13. microchips   15. hacker
17. log on

G. 1. backup   2. microchip   3. glitch   4. network   5. default
6. hard drive   7. scroll   8. software   9. browser   10. hacker

H. (a) Answers will vary. Possible combinations: blinking cursor, Internet browser,
Internet home page; data encryption, backup system, desktop icon, interactive
software, simple upgrade, default browser, default printer, computer upgrade,
computer software, computer application, network software, network application,
network system

(b) Answers will vary.

I.   Answers will vary.

Unit 5

A. 1. i   2. l   3. j   4. g   5. f   6. k   7. h   8. e   9. a   10. b
11. c   12. d

B. 1. (the) water table   2. carcinogen   3. reclaimed it   4. erupt   5. habitat
6. lava   7. survivor   8. pesticide   9. radiation   10. detergent
11. smoggy   12. ozone layer   13. biodegradable

C. 1. T   2. F   3. T   4. F   5. F   6. T   7. T   8. F   9. F
10. T   11. T

D. 1. ozone   2. inhabitant   3. uniqueness   4. monitor   5. quiet   6. fill
7. enlarge   8. survivor   9. survival   10. review   11. reclamation

E. 1. extinction   2. smog   3. detergent   4. lava   5. ozone layer
6. carcinogen   7. diversity   8. radiation   9. filter   10. diversity
11. endanger   12. monitor   13. recycle

F. 1. giving rise to   2. extinction   3. eruption   4. volcanoes
5. biodiversity   6. habitats   7. niches   8. niches   9. endangered
10. extinct   11. food chain   12. pesticides   13. survive
14. reclamation   15. recycling   16. monitoring

G. **Across** 1. biodegradable   4. extinct   6. reclaim   7. give rise
    11. survivor   13. endangered   14. filter   17. carcinogen   19. habitat
    21. ozone layer   22. niches   24. detergent

   Down 2. recycle   3. lava   5. pesti   8. irradiate   9. herbi
    10. biodiversity   12. erupt   15. food chain   16. monitor   18. table
    20. volcano   23. smog

H. 1. pesticide   2. protected   3. treaty   4. religious, ethnic   5. land
    6. high   7. ash   8. warning   9. biodegradable   10. high on
    11. coffee, water

I. 1. survivors   2. residue   3. detergent   4. extinct   5. religious
    6. filtered   7. monitor   8. layer   9. habitat   10. niche   11. volcanic
    12. warning   13. carcinogen   14. (a) species (b) extinct   15. recycling
    16. reclamation

J . Answers will vary.

Unit 6

A. 1. e   2. h   3. f   4. i   5. j   6. k   7. l   8. a   9. d   10. b
    11. g   12. c

B. 1. humanities   2. anthology   3. plagiarizing   4. collaborating
    5. pedagogy   6. electives   7. dissertation   8. facilitating   9. transcript
    10. commencement

C. 1. F   2. F   3. T   4. F   5. T   6. T   7. F   8. T   9. F
    10. T

D. 1. mentor, guide   2. anthology, collection   3. plagiarize, copy   4. marginal,
    minimal   5. profile, description   6. redundant, repetitive   7. ease, facilitate
    8. sabbatical, break   9. cooperate, collaborate   10. mainstream, include

E. 1. c   2. e   3. c   4. e   5. b   6. c, d

F. 1. commencement   2. profiles   3. accredited   4. framework
    5. practicum   6. anachronistic   7. collaborate   8. mentor
    9. humanities   10. curriculum *or* curricular   11. transcript
    12. curriculum   13. electives   14. marginal   15. minor
    16. facilitate   17. dissertation   18. commencement   19. ivory tower

G. 1. made   2. partner   3. provide, useful, for   4. in, with
   5. serve on, an, basis   6. official, copy   7. taking   8. emphasis
   9. practice of   10. address   11. from   12. a degree in the

H. 1. c   2. b   3. a   4. c   5. d   6. b   7. b   8. d

I. 1. a   2. b   3. b   4. a   5. b   6. a   7. a   8. b

J. Answers will vary.

Unit 7

A. 1. l   2. h   3. g   4. j   5. a   6. k   7. i   8. c   9. f   10. d
   11. b   12. e

B. 1. transfusion   2. cast   3. preventive   4. crutches   5. pediatricians
   6. autopsy   7. joints   8. sterile   9. critical care, intensive care
   10. fracture

C. 1. b, d   2. a, e   3. b, e   4. b, d   5. a, c, e

D. 1. F   2. F   3. T   4. F   5. T   6. T   7. F   8. F   9. T
   10. F

E. 1. transfusion   2. clinic   3. joint   4. cardiac   5. paramedic
   6. fracture   7. sterile   8. pediatrician

F. 1. inflamed   2. tumor   3. outpatient   4. side effect   5. paramedic
   6. contagious   7. transfusion

G. 1. paramedics   2. stabilized   3. transfusion   4. specialist   5. cardiac
   6. pediatrician   7. critically   8. sprained   9. fractured   10. cast
   11. crutches   12. clinic   13. clinic   14. checkup   15. preventive
   16. side effects   17. inflammation   18. joints   19. outpatient

H. (a)1. common   2. aching   3. care unit   4. compound   5. highly
   6. local   7. yearly   8. nurse   9. ankle

   (b) Answers will vary.

I. 1. listed in critical condition   2. preventive approach   3. autopsy report
    4. cardiac arrest   5. sterile procedures   6. hobbling on crutches
    7. outpatient therapy   8. benign tumor   9. emergency transfusion
    10. plaster cast

J. Answers will vary.

Unit 8

A. 1. h   2. e   3. i   4. c   5. f   6. l   7. a   8. k   9. d   10. j
   11. b   12. g

B. 1. alternatives   2. genres   3. figurative   4. omniscient   5. distinguishable
   6. proverb   7. lucidly

C. 1. anticlimactic   2. copyright   3. classic   4. articulately   5. attributing
   6. realistic

D. 1. F   2. F   3. T   4. T   5. T   6. F   7. F   8. T   9. T
   10. F

E. 1. alternate   2. impressive   3. description   4. return   5. support
   6. seriously   7. explicit   8. brilliant   9. manner   10. contemporary
   11. satirically   12. connotation

F. 1. satire   2. ironic   3. connotations   4. analogy   5. anecdote
   6. classic   7. omniscient   8. critical of   9. attribute   10. proverbs
   11. realistically   12. viable

G. 1. anticlimax   2. colloquial   3. respond   4. pathos   5. articulating
   6. alternative   7. lucidity

H. Answers may vary in how they are expressed. Example answers:
   1. The twins were so similar that I was unable to say which was which.
   2. Shakespeare is by far the greatest dramatist.
   3. Big businesses sometimes employ specialists to motivate their workers by giving
      them talks.
   4. If someone breaks copyright laws, he or she may be charged with a crime and
      punished by being fined or imprisoned.

I. 1. clear articulation   2. omniscient god   3. not just a figure of speech
    4. popular genres   5. personal attributes   6. speaking ironically
    7. economically viable   8. flash of inspiration   9. copyrighted material

J.   1. (a) anecdotes (b) satirical   2. proverbs   3. (a) classic (b) responded
     4. colloquial   5. pathetic   6. realistic

K.   (a)1. consider   2. highly   3. to   4. negative   5. barely   6. conclude
     7. lucid   8. to

     (b) Answers will vary.

L.   (a) and (b) Answers will vary.

Unit 9

A. 1. e   2. b   3. d   4. a   5. c

B. 1. a, b, c, d   2. b, c   3. b, c   4. d   5. a, b, c   6. c, d   7. b, c, d
    8. b, d   9. a, b   10. a, d

C. 1. F   2. T   3. T   4. T   5. F   6. T   7. T   8. F   9. T

D. 1. divergent   2. forget   3. antibody   4. microscope   5. hybrid
    6. degenerative

E. 1. compound   2. convergence   3. hormone   4. vaccination *or* immunization
    5. embed   6. microscope   7. reproduce   8. virus *or* parasite
    9. stimulate   10. hybrid   11. degenerate   12. encompass

F. 1. parasite   2. antibody   3. by secretion   4. organism   5. respire
    6. embedding   7. deriving   8. reproduce

G. 1. stimulate, immune, antibodies, bacterial, viral (in either order),
        vaccinate *or* immunize
    2. secretions, hormones
    3. converge, diverge (in either order), degenerate
    4. organisms, comprises
    5. hybrids, inherit, divergent, reproduce
    6. microscope, organisms, bacteria, microscopes

H. **Across** 2. embed   3. hybrid   5. stimulus   6. derive   8. encompassed
    10. hormone   12. parasite   14. degenerate   15. virus   16. respire
    18. organism   20. compound   21. microscopic   22. bacteria

    Down 1. heredity   4. immune   7. vaccines   9. converge   10. he
    11. reproduce   13. antibody   14. divergent   17. comprise
    19. secretion

I. (a) 1. infection, aerobic   2. response   3. rate, artificial   4. AIDS
    5. replacement, therapy

    (b) Answers will vary.

J. 1. response   2. bacterial *or* viral   3. vigor   4. vaccine   5. convergent
    6. degenerative   7. arrest *or* failure   8. hormone, therapy   9. immune
    10. hereditary   11. degenerate

K. Answers will vary.

Unit 10

A. 1. e   2. i   3. h   4. k   5. g   6. a   7. j   8. c   9. d   10. f
    11. b

B. 1. amnesty   2. agitating   3. aristocrats   4. boycotting   5. statesman
    6. dictatorial *or* tyrannical *or* totalitarian   7. canvassing   8. federation
    9. impeachment   10. mandate   11. so-called   12. veto

C. 1. b, e   2. b, c, f   3. d   4. b, c   5. a, d, e

D. 1. T   2. F   3. F   4. F   5. T   6. F   7. T   8. F   9. T
    10. T   11. F   12. F

E. 1. tyranny *or* dictatorship   2. so-called   3. monarch *or* sovereign
    4. forthcoming   5. federate   6. aristocrat

F. 1. anarchic   2. imprisonment   3. allot   4. constituent   5. permit
    6. agitator   7. aristocrat   8. constituency

G. 1. statesmanlike, forthcoming 2. allotted, mandatory 3. boycotts, institutionalized

H. 1. allotted equally to   2. fell into anarchy   3. tyrannical behavior
    4. seek a mandate from   5. threatened a veto   6. member of the aristocracy
    7. declared an amnesty   8. national sovereignty   9. imposes a boycott
    10. statesmanlike behavior   11. best-case scenario   12. Military dictatorships
    13. canvass opinions

I. (a) 1. risk of   2. political   3. voters   4. respected   5. international
    6. grounds for   7. research   8. hereditary   9. union   10. rule
    11. evil

    (b) Answers will vary.

J. 1. b   2. a   3. b   4. b   5. a

K. Answers will vary.

Unit 11

A. 1. c   2. i   3. e   4. l   5. g   6. a   7. j   8. d   9. h   10. k
   11. f   12. b

B. 1. alienated   2. sentimental   3. (by) networking   4. interpersonal
   5. syndrome   6. hypnosis   7. disclosing (them)
   8. morale *or* outlook *or* mind-set

C. 1. ADV   2. V   3. ADJ   4. V   5. ADJ   6. ADJ   7. N   8. N *or* V
   9. N   10. ADV   11. V   12. ADV   13. N   14. ADJ   15. V

D. 1. F   2. F   3. T   4. F   5. T   6. F   7. T   8. T

E. 1. disclose   2. same   3. rehearse   4. learned   5. dumb
   6. procrastinate   7. conform   8. fact

F. 1. morale   2. scrutinizing   3. interpersonal   4. alienated   5. outlook
   6. insomnia

G. **Across** 1. interpersonal   9. sentiment   10. merger   11. scrutiny
   13. intellect   15. deviation   16. network   17. disparate   19. outlook
   21. hypnosis   22. mind-set

   Down 1. insomnia   2. ego   3. procrastinate   4. subliminal
   5. alienate   6. disclose   7. delusion   8. primal   12. reconstruct
   14. morale   18. syndrome   20. bias

H. 1. gender ~~toward~~ bias   2. the merger of . . . ~~between~~ and
   3. positive ~~distant~~ outlook   4. Down ~~disease~~ syndrome   5. flatter ~~up~~ their egos
   6. morale . . . was at ~~solid~~ rock bottom   7. failure ~~not~~ to disclose
   8. reconstruct the ~~actions~~ events   9. wide disparity ~~distance~~ between
   10. proper ~~of~~ mind-set

I. 1. interpersonal skills   2. closely scrutinize *or* carefully scrutinize
   3. old-boy network   4. under the delusion   5. sharpen one's intellect
   6. sharp deviation   7. growing sentiment   8. keep on procrastinating

J. Answers will vary.

Unit 12

A. 1. d 2. g 3. j 4. a 5. l 6. b 7. m 8. p 9. c 10. n
11. q 12. e 13. h 14. o 15. k 16. f 17. i

B. 1. hypothesis 2. cause 3. constraint 4. correlation 5. quantitatively
6. inductive 7. confirm *or* validate 8. subject(s) 9. qualitatively

C. 1. predict 2. qualitative 3. random 4. hypothetical 5. subject
6. confirm 7. significant 8. constraint

D. 1. F 2. F 3. T 4. F 5. F 6. T 7. T 8. T 9. T 10. F
11. T

E. 1. a, d 2. b, d 3. c 4. a, c 5. a, b, d 6. b, d 7. a, c 8. c, d
9. a, b, d 10. a, b

F. 1. experiments 2. equivalent 3. significant 4. criterion
5. predictability 6. demonstration 7. correlation 8. confirmed
9. predicted 10. reliability 11. demonstration 12. experiment
13. validating 14. significant 15. experimental 16. variable

G. 1. roughly, degree 2. final 3. independent 4. established
5. sole 6. logical 7. conducting, double-blind (with **experiment**), subject
(with **experimental**) 8. well-established (with **hypothesis**), predictive (with
validity) 9. period 10. reliable, weather 11. full, grasped
12. advantage 13. manipulate (with **variable**), experimental (with **subjects**)

H. 1. relationship 2. practical 3. faulty 4. beyond our
5. referenced tests 6. built-in 7. establish 8. analysis
9. obvious *or* safe

I. Answers will vary.

Unit 13

A. 1. a, d 2. c, d 3. b, c 4. a, b 5. c, d 6. b, d 7. a, b 8. c
9. d 10. c

B. 1. elastic 2. volatile 3. base 4. chaos 5. decompose 6. molecule
7. equation 8. reflection 9. eclipse 10. evaporate 11. volatile

C. 1. spontaneous   2. equilibrium   3. ionic   4. nucleus   5. solvent
   6. aromatic   7. lens   8. chain reaction   9. catalyst   10. diffusion
   11. balance   12. equate   13. inertia   14. solution   15. equilibrium
   16. diffuse

D. 1. T   2. T   3. F   4. F   5. F   6. F   7. T   8. T   9. T   10. F
   11. T   12. T

E. 1. g   2. j   3. k   4. f   5. i   6. e   7. d   8. b   9. c   10. h
   11. a

F. 1. Nuclear   2. fission   3. fusion   4. decomposition   5. cohesive
   6. fusion   7. inhibit   8. nuclear   9. spontaneously   10. chaos

G. **Across** 2. prism   5. spontaneous   7. equilibrium   12. molecular
   14. catalytic   16. of   19. nuclear   20. inert   21. lens   23. equation
   25. chaos   26. ions   27. chain

   Down 1. diffuse   3. inhibit   4. momentum   6. solvent   7. evaporate
   8. aromatic   9. reflection   10. solution   11. decompose   13. volatile
   15. cohere   17. fusion   18. elastic   22. fission   24. basic

H. 1. strong solvent   2. dilute solution   3. cohesive force   4. gaseous diffusion
   5. contact lenses   6. catalytic converters   7. organic solvents
   8. emotional equilibrium   9. volatile liquid   10. evaporative cooling
   11. reflective coatings   12. Nuclear fusion   13. nuclear energy
   14. nuclear chain reaction   15. nuclear energy   16. fission reactor
   17. atomic nuclei   18. fission products

I. 1. b   2. a   3. a   4. b   5. c   6. b   7. a

J. 1. liquid   2. combustion   3. strong, organic
   4. dilute (with **solution**), strongly (with **basic**)   5. compounds
   6. material, light   7. structure   8. grind

K. Answers will vary.

Unit 14

A. 1. i   2. h   3. g   4. j   5. f   6. c   7. l   8. b   9. a   10. k
   11. d   12. e

B. 1. bigoted   2. dialogue   3. double standard   4. heterogeneous
   5. hierarchy   6. status quo   7. prestigious

C. 1. F   2. F   3. T   4. T   5. F   6. T   7. F   8. F   9. F   10. T

D. 1. g   2. i   3. a   4. b   5. j   6. d   7. c   8. e   9. f   10. h

E. 1. dialogue   2. domain   3. double standard   4. conformed   5. latent
   6. veritable   7. prestigious   8. principles

F. 1. domain   2. mobile   3. veritable   4. dialogue(s)   5. status quo
   6. hierarchy

G. 1. gender   2. had *or* applied   3. withdraw   4. latent   5. bigotry
   6. dialogue   7. prestige   8. culture *or* community *or* way of life
   9. upwardly   10. stereotype

H. 1. b   2. a   3. a   4. b   5. a   6. b   7. a   8. b   9. b   10. a

I.   Answers will vary.

Words in Volumes 1–7

Numbers refer to volume and unit. A word with no numbers following it is one of the 600 words assumed known for Volume 1. The letter "p" or "r" after a Volume 7 entry indicates whether the word is in the *Words for Production* or *Words for Recognition* section of the unit.

a
a lot of
abandon, 5-6
abate, 7-16r
abbreviation, 3-5
aberrant, 7-21p
abet, 7-7r
abhor, 7-16r
able
abolish, 5-1
abominable, 7-14r
about
about, 3-7
above, 2-8
abroad, 2-22
abrogate, 7-7r
abrupt, 3-5
absent
absent, 2-1
absolutely, 5-8
absorb, 6-3
abstain, 7-13p
abstract, 4-23
absurd, 7-12p, 7-19r
abundance, 6-15

abuse, 6-9
abyss, 7-21p
academic, 3-23
accelerate, 5-19
accept, 1-1, 6-18
acceptable, 6-18
access, 5-6
accident, 2-10
accommodate, 6-13
accompany, 4-18
accomplish, 3-2
accomplished, 7-19r
according to, 2-11
account, 2-12
account for, 6-16
accumulate, 4-22
accurate, 3-13
accuse, 5-10
accustomed to, 3-8
achieve, 3-23
acid, 3-10
acquaintance, 5-17
acquiesce, 7-2r
acquire, 4-22
acre, 5-7

act, 2-23
action, 3-9
activity, 3-12
actually, 4-3
acumen, 7-19r
acute, 6-17
adamant, 7-2p
adapt, 2-22
add, 2-12
add up, 6-13
addict, 5-8
address, 1-6, 6-1
adept, 7-19r
adequate, 4-7
adjacent, 6-13
adjust, 4-4
administrator, 4-1
admire, 3-21
admit, 3-1, 5-25
admonish, 7-4r
adolescent, 7-4p
adopt, 6-5, 7-4p
adore, 7-17r
adult, 3-14
adultery, 7-17p

advanced, 2-1

advantage, 1-12

adventure, 3-20

adversary, 7-3r

adverse, 6-23, 7-2p

advertisement, 2-17

advise, 4-1

advocate, 5-1

affair, 5-22

affairs, 5-22

affection, 5-17

affluent, 5-6

afford, 3-8

afraid, 2-18

after

afternoon, 1-15

afterward, 3-15

again

against, 3-9

age

age, 2-5

agency, 4-12

agent, 4-12

aggressive, 6-12

agitate for, 7-20r

ago

agony, 6-17

agree(ment), 3-18

agriculture, 2-13

ahead, 5-14

aid, 4-12

aim, 5-8

aimless, 7-12p

air

air force, 1-18

airmail, 3-5

airplane, 1-2

airport, 1-2

alarm, 4-15

alcohol, 4-16

alcoholism, 4-16

alcove, 7-18r

alert, 3-9

alibi, 7-1p

alien, 5-22

align, 7-7p

alike, 5-17

alive, 3-19

all

allergy, 5-23

allow, 1-8

ally, 6-18

almost

almost, 3-1

alone, 2-5

along, 4-24

aloud, 3-22

already

also

alter, 3-4

alternate, 6-15

although, 3-14

altitude, 3-8

always

amateur, 3-21

amaze, 4-20

ambassador, 1-20

ambiguous, 5-24

ambition, 1-14

amble, 7-21r

ambulance, 1-16

ambush, 7-3p

amend, 4-1

ammunition, 6-20

among, 2-5

amount, 3-15

amphibian, 7-8p

ample, 6-6

amusement, 2-23

an

analyze, 5-12

anarchy, 7-20p

anatomy, 7-22p

ancestor, 4-18

anchor, 6-8

ancient, 2-22

and

anesthetic, 6-17

angel, 4-20

anger, 3-14

angle, 4-2

animal

animosity, 7-3r

ankle, 3-19

annex, 7-5p

anniversary, 2-5

announce, 3-24

annoy, 5-10

annual, 2-2

annul, 7-7r

anonymous, 6-12

another

answer

anthropology , 5-5

anticipate, 5-2

antidote, 6-17

antique, 4-7

any

anybody

anyone

anything

anywhere

apartment, 1-3

apology, 3-18

appalling, 7-14r

apparatus, 5-5

apparel, 7-11r

apparent, 5-2

appeal, 6-12

appear(ance), 3-4

appease, 7-2r, 7-15r

appendix, 6-10

appetite, 3-15

applause, 5-18

apple

application, 5-14

applied, 6-7

apply, 1-1

appoint, 4-3

appreciate, 6-9

apprehend, 7-14r

apprentice, 7-6p

approach, 5-1

appropriate for, 2-9

approve (of), 3-14

approximately, 2-22

April

apt, 7-6p

aptitude, 7-6p

aquatic, 7-8p

arbitration, 6-16

architect, 6-13

ardor, 7-17r

are

area, 2-3, 5-12

argue, 3-2

arise, 6-4

arm

armistice, 7-3r

arms

arms, 5-9

army, 1-18

around, 1-19

arraign, 7-14r

arrange, 5-22

arrangement, 2-22

arrest, 2-7

arrive

arson, 5-21

article, 2-17, 5-25

artificial, 6-3

artist, 1-14

as

as a rule, 6-14

ascertain, 7-12r

ash, 5-21

ashamed, 4-9

ask

aspect, 4-21

asphyxiate, 7-22r

aspiration, 7-19p

assailant, 7-1r

assassinate, 7-1p

assault, 7-1p

assemble, 4-16

assembly, 4-16

assent, 7-2r

assess, 6-16

asset, 4-22

assiduous, 7-2r

assign(ment), 1-8

assign, 3-24

assist, 3-24

associate, 5-13

association, 5-13

assuage, 7-2r, 7-15r

assume, 4-23, 5-18

astonish, 6-8

astronomy, 2-24

astute, 7-19p

asylum, 7-22p

at

at least, 2-22

at once, 3-2

athletic, 3-23

atlas, 6-10

atmosphere, 3-10

atom, 4-13

atrocious, 7-14r

attached, 3-16

attack, 2-7

attain, 4-25

attempt, 1-1

attend, 3-22

attention (pay), 3-1

attic, 5-6

attire, 7-11r

attitude, 3-7, 4-1

attract(ive), 4-10

auction, 7-10p

audience, 1-9

August

aunt

aunt, 2-5

authentic, 6-3

author, 2-17

authority, 4-12

automatic, 5-8

automobile, 1-2

autonomous, 6-1

available, 2-3

avalanche, 7-8p

avarice, 7-10r

avenue, 2-25

average, 3-1

avert, 7-22r

avoid, 2-7

aware, 4-10

awful, 4-9

awkward, 5-19

awning, 7-5p

baby

bachelor, 4-18

back, 1-16

back down, 5-22

back out, 6-23

back up, 5-19, 6-15

background, 6-2

backwards, 3-3

body, 1-16

bog, 7-8r

boil, 2-4

bomb, 2-8

bond, 6-5

bone

book

boot, 1-17

booty, 7-3r

border, 4-12

boring, 1-9

born

borrow, 2-12

boss, 1-5

botany, 4-13

botch, 7-2p

both

bother, 3-9

bottle, 3-15

bottom, 3-6

bound for, 6-11

boundary, 5-16

bowl, 1-15

box

boy

brain, 3-19

brake, 4-24, 5-19

brand, 4-16

brave, 3-20

brawny, 7-15r

bread

break, 1-16

break down, 5-6, 6-7

break in, 5-19, 6-4

break into, 5-10, 6-4

break off, 6-5

break out, 5-23

break up, 5-17, 6-12

breakfast

breathe, 2-6

breed, 6-15

breeze, 5-21

bribe, 4-15

brick, 1-12

bride, 3-14

bridge, 1-11

brief, 5-8

bright, 5-21

brilliant, 5-13

bring

bring, 2-12

bring about, 5-14

bring off, 5-22

bring on, 5-2

bring out, 5-24

bring to, 6-17

bring up, 4-18

broke, 7-10r

brook, 7-8r

broom, 5-21

brother

brown

brush, 5-13

brush off, 6-23

bubble, 5-14

budget, 3-18

build (built)

bulb, 4-7

bulk, 6-14

bullet, 6-12

bully, 7-7p

bungle, 7-2r

bunk, 7-18r

burden, 6-16

bureau, 6-1

bureaucracy, 6-1, 7-20p

burly, 7-15r

burn, 3-15

burn down, 5-21

burn up, 5-21

burst, 3-12

bury, 3-22

bus, 1-2

business, 1-5

busy

busy, 2-5

but

butter, 3-15

button, 4-10

buy (bought)

buy out, 6-15

buy up, 6-6

by

cabin, 2-25, 7-18p

cabinet, 4-7

cafeteria, 1-8

cage, 3-17

cake, 2-4

calamitous, 7-2r

calculate, 3-23

calendar, 2-22

calf, 5-7

call

call for, 6-4

call off, 5-13

call on, 6-1

call up, 6-20

calm, 3-17

calm down, 6-8

calorie, 5-11

camera, 1-7

camouflage, 7-3p

camp, 1-21

campaign, 5-9

campus, 1-8

can

cancel, 2-23

cancer, 4-6

candidate, 3-18

drop in, 5-17

drop out, 5-5

drown, 4-6

drowsy, 7-9r

drug, 5-1

dry, 1-4

due, 3-16, 3-25

dull, 1-25, 6-2

dump, 6-19

durable, 6-6

duration, 6-6

during

dust, 3-16

duty, 3-20

dwell on, 5-6

dwelling, 5-6, 7-5r

dwindle, 7-16r

dye, 4-10

dynamic, 6-8

each

eager, 3-24

ear

early, 1-4

earn, 2-12

earth, 1-23, 5-7

earthquake, 4-8

east

easy

eat

eat up, 6-3

echo, 4-4

ecology, 5-14

economical, 5-5

economics, 5-5

economize, 5-5, 6-3

economy, 5-5, 6-6

edge, 1-11

edict, 7-20r

edifice, 7-5r

edit, 4-5

educate, 2-1

eerie, 7-8p

effect, 5-2

efficient, 2-20

effort, 2-2

egg

eight

elderly, 4-18

elect, 2-11

electricity, 1-3

element, 6-19

elementary, 6-16

elementary school, 1-1

elements, 6-19

elephant

elevator, 3-16

eleven

eliminate, 4-9

else, 1-25

emaciated, 7-9r

embarrassed, 3-9

embassy, 1-20

embezzle, 7-1p

embrace, 7-4p

emerge, 6-25

emergency, 1-24

emigrate, 4-12

emit, 5-12

emotion, 3-14

emphasis, 3-7

empire, 6-18

empirical, 6-24

employ(ee), 1-5

empty, 1-2

emulate, 7-17p

enable, 6-22

enchant, 7-17r

enclose, 5-16

encourage, 4-18

encroach, 7-16r

end

endeavor, 7-15r

endless, 3-8

endure, 6-13

enemy, 1-18

energy, 4-6

enforce, 5-25

enfranchise, 7-7p

engage in, 6-16

engine, 2-10

engineering, 2-19

engulf, 6-19

enjoy, 1-7

enlarge, 5-6

enlist, 5-9

enmity, 7-3r

enormous, 4-11

enough

enough, 2-20

enrage, 5-13

enslave, 6-15

ensure, 6-6

enter

enterprise, 6-16

entertain, 2-23

entertainment, 1-9

enthrall, 7-17r

enthusiasm, 3-21

entire, 3-21, 5-14

entitle, 5-18

envelope, 1-6

environment, 2-16

envy, 3-8

epidemic, 4-6

episode, 5-13

equal, 3-8

equator, 2-15

equipment, 4-1

era, 6-5

formal, 2-9
format, 5-24
formidable, 6-19
formula, 5-12
fort, 6-20
forth
fortress, 7-18p
fortunate, 4-22
fortunately, 1-14
fortune, 4-22
forty
forward(s), 6-22
foster, 7-4p
found, 5-5
foundation, 5-5
fountain, 3-12
four
foyer, 7-18p
fraction, 6-24
fracture, 7-22r
fragile, 5-14
frail, 7-22r
frame, 5-13
frank, 6-5
free
freeze, 2-15
freight, 4-24
frequent, 1-24
fresh, 1-15
friction, 6-7, 7-4r
Friday
friend
frighten, 1-18
from
front
frugal, 7-10r
fruit
frustrate, 5-25
fuel, 2-10
fulfill, 5-5

fulfilling, 5-5
fun, 1-25
fund, 6-14
fundamental, 6-21
funds, 6-14
funeral, 4-20, 6-21
funny, 1-9, 5-16
fur, 3-4
furious, 5-20
furnace, 4-7
furniture, 1-3
furtive, 5-21
furtive, 7-1r
fury, 7-14r
future
future, 2-2

gain, 4-17
gallery, 5-13
gamble, 4-22
game, 1-10, 7-21p
gang, 2-7
gap, 5-24
garage, 1-12, 5-8
garbage, 5-11
garbled, 7-12r
garden
garish, 7-11r
garment, 4-10
garret, 7-5r
garrison, 7-3p
gas, 1-12, 2-15
gasoline, 2-10, 5-19
gasp, 7-22p
gate, 3-16
gather, 4-19
gaudy, 7-11r
gauge, 5-19
gaunt, 7-9r
gaze, 5-20

gear, 5-19
gem, 7-10r
gene, 6-5
genealogy, 6-5
general, 2-11, 4-17
generate, 6-13
generation, 4-18
generous, 6-15
genetics, 6-24
gentle, 4-18
genuine, 3-4
geography, 1-23
geology, 3-10
germ, 4-6
germane, 7-12r
gesture, 6-10
get
get across, 5-24
get ahead, 6-4
get along, 6-5
get around, 5-25
get away, 5-10
get away with, 5-10
get by, 5-7
get down to, 6-16
get in, 5-19
get off, 5-19, 6-22
get on, 5-19, 6-5
get on with, 5-8
get out of, 5-19
get over, 5-23
get through, 6-2
get through with, 6-2
ghetto, 7-5p
ghost, 3-12
giant, 4-17
gift
girder, 7-18r
girl
give

give away, 5-9

give back, 6-20

give in, 6-11

give off, 5-16

give out, 5-22, 6-19

give up, 5-9

glad, 1-7

glade, 7-8r

glance, 5-4

glass, 1-15

glasses, 3-19

glean, 7-12r

glen, 7-21r

glimpse, 7-12r

global, 6-6

globe, 6-6

gloomy, 5-3

gloves, 1-17

glow, 5-21

glue, 3-12

gnaw, 7-13r

go

go back, 6-2

go back on, 5-22

go in for, 5-20

go on, 5-20, 6-2

go out, 6-13

go over, 5-4, 6-22

go through with, 6-2

go with, 5-15

go without, 6-11

goal, 4-25

god, 3-22

gold

golf, 1-9

good

good-bye

goods, 3-25

gorge, 7-13p, 7-21r

gorgeous, 7-11r

gossip, 5-24

government, 1-20

grab, 4-21

grade, 1-8

gradual, 4-3

graduate, 1-1

graduated, 6-14

graft, 7-20r

grain, 3-17

gram

grandfather

grandmother

grant, 6-24

graph, 6-7

grasp, 6-25

grass

grateful, 5-17

grave, 3-22, 6-9

gravity, 2-24

gray, 4-7

great, 4-17

green

greet, 4-23

grief, 4-20

grievance, 7-15r

grim, 6-6, 7-2p

grime, 7-5r

grin, 6-8

grind, 6-15, 7-13p

grip, 5-20

gripe, 7-15r

grocery, 4-14

grotto, 7-21r

ground, 1-23

grounds, 6-5

group, 1-10

grow, 1-19

grow up, 6-5

grudge, 7-14r

grueling, 7-2p

gruesome, 7-12r

grumbles, 7-15r

guarantee, 2-21, 4-22

guard, 1-18

guardian, 7-4p

guerrilla, 6-20

guess, 1-13

guest, 1-12

guilty, 4-15

gulf, 6-19

gully, 7-8r

gun, 1-18

guy, 2-8

habit, 2-9

hair

half

hall, 2-25

hallucinate, 7-22p

halt, 6-20

halting, 6-20

ham, 3-15

hammer, 4-7

hamper, 7-2r

hand

hand down, 5-17, 6-21

hand in, 6-7

hand out, 5-5

hand over, 5-25

hand over, 7-3r

handicap, 5-23

handle, 1-20

handsome

hang, 3-16

hang around, 6-12

hang up, 1-24, 6-22

happen, 2-10

happy

harass, 7-14r

harbor, 5-16

hard, 1-23
hardly, 3, 2-25
hardship, 5-7
harm, 4-9
harmony, 5-17
harsh, 3-11
harvest, 5-7
hat
hate, 1-22
have
have on, 5-15
have over, 6-5
have to
havoc, 7-15p
hay, 2-13
hazard, 6-22, 7-15p
he
head
head, 1-20, 5-24
headline, 2-17
heal, 5-2
health, 1-16
hear
hear from, 5-17
hear of, 6-10
heart, 3-19, 5-20
heartless, 5-20
hearty, 5-20
heat, 1-12
heaven, 3-22
heavy, 1-13
heel, 7-11p
heirloom, 7-17p
helicopter, 1-18
hell, 3-22
help
hem, 7-11p
hemisphere, 3-11
hemorrhage, 7-22r
henceforth, 7-12r

her
herd, 4-11
here
heritage, 6-5
hermit, 7-8p
hero, 5-9
herself
hesitate, 2-22
hide, 4-15
hideous, 7-11r
high
high school, 1-1
highway, 4-24
hill, 1-23
him
himself
hinder, 6-11, 7-2r
hint, 6-10, 7-12p
hire, 2-2
his
history, 2-19
hit
hit on, 5-12
hoard, 7-13p
hoax, 7-12p
hobby, 1-9
hold
hold, 3-15
hold off, 6-1
hold out, 6-20
hold up, 5-25
hole, 3-3
holiday
holler, 7-1r
holy, 3-22
home
honest/honor, 1-20
hook, 6-8
hope
horizon, 5-3

horizontal, 5-3
horn, 1-11
horrible, 1-18
horse
hose, 5-5
hospital
hostility, 6-20, 7-3p
hot
hotel
hour
house
how
however, 3-1
hug, 7-4r
human, 3-9
humble, 5-4
humid, 3-11
hundred
hunger, 2-4
hunt, 3-17
hurricane, 5-16
hurry, 1-11
hurt, 1-16
husband
hut, 6-11
hydroelectric, 6-24
hygiene, 6-17
hypothesis, 5-12

I
ice
idea
ideal, 2-25
identical, 2-5
identify , 4-15
ideology, 7-7p
idiot, 7-6r
idle, 5-18
if
ignite, 6-25

lawyer, 1-14

lay, 3-16

lay in, 5-9

layer, 3-6

lazy, 2-2

lead, 2-10

leaf, 2-18

league, 4-21

leak, 2-16

lean, 6-18, 7-5p

leap, 7-8r

learn

lease, 1-12, 5-18

leather, 1-17

leave, 1-7

leave out, 5-24

lecture, 3-1

ledge, 7-8p

left

leg

legal, 3-9

leisure, 4-25

lend, 2-12

less, 2-2

lesson

let, 3-14

let down, 5-15, 6-21

let out, 5-15, 6-17

let up, 5-3

letter

level, 2-1

lever, 6-7

liberal, 5-1

liberty, 3-18

library

license, 1-14

lid, 2-4

lie, 2-7

lie down, 6-20

lieutenant, 4-17

life

lift, 2-14

light, 1-3, 1-13

light up, 5-21

lightning, 3-11

like

likely, 4-8

limit, 1-13

line, 3-23, 7-11p

lineage, 7-4r

linger, 7-2r

liquid, 2-15

list, 4-5, 7-5r

listen

literature, 3-1

little

live

live down, 5-20

live on, 5-11

live up to, 6-21

livestock, 5-7

load, 3-3

loan, 4-22

loathe, 7-16r

lobby, 1-21

local, 1-24

location, 2-3

lock/unlock, 2-7

loft, 7-5r

logical, 2-24

lonely, 2-22

long

longitude, 5-3

look

look after, 5-7

look back on, 5-7

look down on, 6-21

look forward to, 5-13

look into, 5-10

look over, 5-8

look up, 5-24

look up to, 5-20

loose, 3-4

loot, 7-3p

Lord, 4-20

lose/loss, 1-10

lot, 6-13

loud, 2-10

lousy, 5-3

love

low, 1-14

loyal, 3-20

lucid, 7-6r

luck, 3-24

luggage, 1-7

lunch

lungs, 4-6

lurid, 7-12p

lurk, 7-1p

luxury, 4-4

machine

mad, 3-21

magazine

magic, 3-12

magnet, 6-24

magnitude, 6-25

maid, 1-14

mail

main, 4-2

maintenance, 4-7

major, 2-16, 2-19, 5-9

majority, 3-18

make (made)

make out, 6-7, 6-14

make up, 5-13, 5-17, 6-16

malady, 7-9r

male

male, 5-23

malevolence, 7-14r

malice, 7-14p
mammal, 6-7
mammoth, 7-21r
man (men)
manager, 2-25
mankind, 4-13
mannequin, 7-11p
manner, 6-11
manners, 6-11
mansion, 7-5p
manual, 4-25
manufacture, 3-2
many
map
march, 2-8
marine, 3-10
mark, 4-6
mark (grade), 4-23
market, 2-13
marry
marsh, 7-8r
martyr, 7-16p
mass, 3-10
master, 4-23
match, 3-21, 5-21
material, 2-9
maternal, 6-5
mathematics, 2-19
matter, 4-22, 6-10
mature, 6-5
maximum, 3-13
may
maybe
mayor, 5-1
me
meager, 7-15p
mean
mean, 5-5
mean to, 5-18
means, 5-5
measure, 2-15, 5-1

meat
mechanic, 6-7
mechanical, 6-7
media, 2-17
medicine
medium, 5-6
meet
melody, 6-8
melt, 2-15
member, 2-5
memorial, 4-17
memorize, 4-17
memory, 4-17
menace, 5-22
menial, 7-15p
mental, 3-12
mention, 5-4
mercenary, 7-3p
merchant, 4-14
mercy, 6-21
merely, 6-22
merit, 6-16
message, 1-24
meter
method, 2-16
metric, 3-10
middle, 1-11
midnight, 1-22
midwife, 7-22p
might
migrant, 6-15
mild, 4-8
mile, 3-5
military, 1-18
milk
mill, 6-15
million
million, 3-5
mince, 7-13r
mind, 3-23, 3-11
mine, 4-9

minimum, 3-13
minion, 7-2r
minister, 6-18
minority, 3-18
minus, 4-13
minute
miracle, 3-22
mirror, 1-17
miscarriage, 7-22p
misdemeanor, 7-1p
miserable, 6-13
misgiving, 7-15r
Miss
miss, 2-1
missile, 6-20
mission, 6-21
mist, 7-8p
mistake
misuse, 5-14
mix, 5-11
mobility, 5-18
model, 3-12
moderate, 6-6
modern, 2-10
modest, 3-21
modify, 6-23
moist, 5-3
molest, 7-14p
mollify, 7-2p
monetary, 6-14
money
monogamy, 7-17p
monopolize, 6-16
monopoly, 6-16
month
monthly, 2-2
mood, 5-2
moon
moral, 5-21
morals, 5-21
more

moreover, 6-23

morning

mortal, 4-20

most

motel, 1-7

mother

motion, 4-2

motive, 5-25

motor, 3-3

mount, 6-11

mountain

mouth

move

move, 1-11

movement, 6-4

movies

Mr.

Mrs.

much

mud, 1-23

mulish, 7-17r

multiply, 2-12

mumble, 7-6p

munch, 7-13r

municipal, 6-1

murder, 1-22

muscle, 4-21

muse, 7-6r

museum, 2-22

music

must

mutter, 7-6r

mutual, 5-17

my

myself

mystery, 1-22

myth, 6-21

nail, 4-7

naked, 3-4

name

narrative, 6-2

narrow, 2-10

nation, 3-20

native, 4-4

natural, 2-14

nausea, 7 -9p

navy, 1-18

near

nearby, 2-3, 4-14

neat, 4-1

necessary

necessary, 3-1

neck, 3-19

need

needle, 4-10

needy, 7-10r

negative, 3-7

neglect, 5-17

negotiate, 3-2

neighbor

neighborhood, 1-3

neither, 3-7

nephew, 2-5

nest, 4-19

net, 6-8

never

nevertheless, 6-23

new

news

newspaper

next

nice

niece, 2-5

night

nightmare, 3-12

no

no one

nobility, 7-20p

nobody

nod, 4-24

noise

noise, 2-1

nominate, 7-7p

nonflammable, 5-21

nonsense, 5-24

noon, 1-8

normal, 3-19

north

nose

not

note, 2-1

nothing

notice, 4-8

notion, 6-8, 7-6r

notorious, 7-14p

nourishment, 6-3

novel, 3-1, 6-10

novice, 7-6r

now

nowadays, 2-20

nowhere

nucleus, 5-12

nude, 5-15

nullify, 7-7r

numb, 7-9p

number

numerous, 3-12

nurse, 1-14, 5-7

nursery, 6-2

nursery school, 6-2

nurture, 7-4p

nut, 4-16

nutritious, 5-11

oaf, 7-6r

obese, 7-22r

obey, 4-17

object, 2-21, 3-6, 6-4

objective, 6-10

obligation, 5-17

obliterate, 7-16p

observe, 5-25
obstacle, 4-21
obstinate, 7-17r
obstreperous, 7-19r
obtain, 4-14
obvious, 2-20
occasion, 3-25
occupation, 3-2
occupy, 4-4, 6-20
occur, 2-10, 4-17
ocean
o'clock
odd, 1-25, 6-14
odds, 5-20
odor, 6-3
of
of course, 2-21
off
offend, 5-17
offer, 3-2
office
officer, 2-8, 6-12, 6-16
official, 2-11
offspring, 6-15
often
oil, 2-16, 5-11
ointment, 7-9p
old
ominous, 7-22p
omit, 5-4
on
once
one
only
onset, 7-9r
onslaught, 7-16p
open
operation, 4-17
operator, 1-24
opinion, 1-20

opportunity, 5-13
opposition, 3-18
oppress, 6-4
optics, 6-24
optimistic, 4-3
optimum, 5-3
optional, 4-1
or
orally, 5-2
orange, 3-11
orchestra, 1-9
ordeal, 7-14p
order, 2-11, 2-21, 5-15
ordinary, 3-25
ore, 6-9
organ, 6-17
organic, 6-24
organize, 4-19
oriental, 3-22
orientation, 4-1
original, 2-21
orphan, 4-18
ostentatious, 7-11p
other
otherwise, 3-25
ought to, 3-14
ounce, 1-13
our
ours
ourselves
out
out of stock, 4-14
outcome, 5-9
outdoors, 1-10
outgrowth, 7-7r
outlay, 7-10p
outlet, 6-9
output, 4-3
outside, 1-6
outstanding, 6-2

oven, 2-4
over
overall, 6-11
overcome, 6-6
overdue, 7-10p
overnight, 1-7
overseas, 1-6
overthrow, 7-7p
overwhelm, 6-16
owe, 3-13
owing to, 6-23
own, 2-2
oxygen, 3-21

pace, 4-23
package, 1-13
page
pain, 1-16
painstaking, 7-12p
paint, 2-3
pair, 1-17
palace, 7-5p
pale, 4-6
pan, 5-11
pan out, 6-6
panel, 6-10
panic, 5-25
pant, 7-22r
pantry, 7-5p
paper
parade, 1-18
paragraph, 2-17
parallel, 5-19
paralysis, 7-9p
parent
park, 1-2, 1-9
parliament, 6-1
part
part, 5-17
partially, 6-9

recommend, 4-8
record, 4-1
recover, 4-6
recreation, 1-9
rectangle, 4-13
recuperate, 7-9r
recur, 5-23
red
reduce, 2-21
refer, 5-24
referendum, 7-20p
reflect, 5-24
reform, 5-1
reformatory, 7-1r
refrigerator, 2-4
refuge, 6-20, 7-5r
refugee, 6-20
refuse, 5-1
regard, 5-24
regarding, 5-24
regardless, 5-24
regime, 6-1, 7-20p
region, 5-7
register, 4-1
regularly, 3-5
regulate, 5-1
rehearsal, 5-13
reject, 4-23
related, 2-5
relative, 4-14
relax, 2-22
release, 5-10
relevant, 6-7, 5-24
relief, 5-23
religion, 3-22
relinquish, 7-3r
reluctant, 3-11
rely (on), 3-14
remain, 4-19
remark, 6-25

remarkable, 6-25
remedy, 6-17
remember
remind, 4-8
remote, 7-8p
remove, 3-4
rendezvous, 7-16r
renew, 6-10
renovate, 7-5p
renown, 7-19r
rent, 1-3
repair, 2-25
repay, 3-13
repeat
replace, 4-19
reply to, 1-13
report, 4-5
represent, 3-18
reprimand, 7-4r
reprisal, 7-3r
republic, 6-18
repulse, 6-20
reputation, 4-5
request, 3-25
require, 1-8
rescind, 7-7r
rescue, 4-19
research, 3-10
resemble, 5-17
reservation, 6-6
residence, 2-25, 7-5r
resign, 3-24
resist, 5-9
resolution, 6-1
resource, 4-11
respect, 1-14, 6-6
responsible, 2-11, 5-8
rest, 2-6
restaurant, 1-15
restrain, 6-21

restriction, 4-12
result, 2-24
resume, 5-23
retaliate, 7-3p
retard, 7-6p
retarded, 7-6p
retire, 4-3
retreat, 5-9
retribution, 7-1r
return
reveal, 3-7
revenge, 7-1p
revenue, 6-1, 7-10p
reverse, 5-22
review, 3-1
revise, 5-24
revive, 7-9p
revoke, 7-7p
revolt, 6-20, 7-20r
revolting, 6-20
revolve, 6-12
revolver, 6-12
reward, 6-12
rhythm, 6-8
rice
rich
ride, 1-19
ridiculous, 5-13
rifle, 5-10
right
right, 5-1
rigid, 6-4
ring, 1-8, 1-24
rinse, 7-11p
riot, 7-14p
riotous, 7-14p
rip, 5-18
ripe, 6-3
rise, 3-8
risk, 3-20

seek to, 6-23

seem, 3-19

seize, 6-20

seldom, 4-14

select, 3-20

selfish, 4-18

sell

seminar, 3-1

send

send back, 6-18

senile, 6-17

senior, 2-19, 5-9

sensational, 7-12p

sense, 5-23

sensible, 5-23

sensitive, 5-23

sentence, 2-17, 5-10

sentry, 7-3r

separate, 3-6

series, 4-14

serious, 3-11

servant, 4-14

serve, 3-20

set, 5-21

set up, 5-16

settle, 4-11

settle on, 5-6

settle up, 6-14

seven

sever, 7-7r

several, 2-9

severe, 3-11

sew, 4-10

sewer, 5-6

sex, 5-23

shade, 3-11

shadow, 2-15

shake, 4-16

shallow, 3-12

shame, 5-14

shape, 4-13, 5-2

share, 2-13, 7-10p

sharp, 3-15, 4-6

she

shed, 7-5p

sheep, 1-19

sheer, 7-8r

sheet, 4-8

shelf, 2-25

shell, 4-19, 6-19

shelter, 4-7

shift, 6-25, 7-2p

shine, 1-4

ship

shirt

shock, 5-13, 6-8

shocking, 5-13

shoe

shoot, 1-22

shop

shore, 1-23

short

shortage, 5-6

should

shoulder, 5-2

shout, 1-22, 7-1r

show

show off, 5-15

show up, 6-25

shred, 7-13p

shrewd, 7-19r

shrink, 4-10

shut

shut off, 6-7

shy, 1-25

sibling, 5-17

sick

side

side, 1-11

sidewalk, 3-5

siege, 7-3p

sight, 3-8

sign, 2-21, 2-25, 3-35

signal, 3-3

significant, 4-5, 6-10

signify, 6-10

silent, 2-7

silly, 5-18

silver, 3-13

similar, 2-20

simple, 3-6

simultaneous, 6-8

sin, 3-22

since, 3-11

sincere, 5-4

sing

single, 2-5

sink, 2-8, 2-25

sister

sit

site, 5-6

situation, 4-17

six

size, 2-3

skeptical, 7-12r

skill, 1-14

skimpy, 7-15r

skin, 3-19

skinny, 7-9r

skirt, 1-17

skulk, 7-1r

sky, 1-4

slave, 6-15

sleep

slide, 3-12

slight, 3-25

slip, 4-8

slope, 6-8

slow

slow down, 6-22

slow up, 6-22

small

smart, 3-23

smell, 3-15

smile

smoke, 2-16

smooth, 3-12

smother, 7-22r

snack, 5-11

snake, 2-18

sneak, 5-22

snow

so

soap

sob, 7-4r

sober, 7-13p

soccer, 2-14

socialism, 5-1

society, 4-12

sock, 2-9

soft, 4-8

soil, 4-11

solar, 4-9

soldier, 1-18

sole, 7-11p

solemn, 7-2r

solid, 2-15

solution, 3-6

solvent, 7-10p

somber, 7-2r

some

somebody

somehow

someone

something

sometimes

somewhere

son

song

soon

sophisticated, 6-7

sore, 5-8, 5-23

sorry

sort, 5-5

sound, 2-23

soup

source, 3-17

south

space, 1-12, 6-24

spank, 7-4p

spare, 6-13

spark, 5-21

sparse, 6-15, 7-15r

speak

special, 2-12

species, 5-16

specify, 4-14

specimen, 6-24

speculate, 7-10p, 7-19p

speech, 1-20

speed, 3-3

spell

spell out, 6-10

spend

sphere, 6-24

spill, 4-19

spirit, 4-20

spiritual, 4-20

spite, 7-14r

split, 6-22

spoil, 7-13p

spoils, 7-3r

sponsor, 6-2

spoon

sport

spot, 3-4, 5-21

spouse, 7-17p

spread, 6-3

spring

spring, 7-8r

spring up, 5-13

squabble, 7-14r

squad, 7-16r

squat, 7-18p

squirm, 7-19p

stable, 4-12

staff, 3-2

stage, 5-18

stain, 5-15

stairs, 2-25

stale, 7-13p

stalk, 7-8p

stamina, 7-22r

stammer, 7-12r

stamp, 1-6

stand

stand by, 5-21

stand for, 6-10

stand out, 6-16

stand up, 6-5, 6-19

stand up for, 6-1

stand up to, 6-1

standard, 4-14

standpoint, 6-10

staple, 7-13p

star, 4-19

stare, 2-23

start

starve, 5-11

state, 3-2, 5-1

station, 1-2, 6-22

statistics, 5-12

status, 6-20

stay, 1-7

steady, 4-8

steal, 1-22

stealthy, 5-21

steel, 4-2

steep, 4-24

step, 3-16

symmetrical, 5-13

sympathize, 5-1

symptom, 5-2

synthesis, 5-15

synthetic, 5-15

system, 2-24

table

table, 5-12

tablet, 7-9r

tactic, 6-20

tail, 3-17

tailor, 7-11p

tainted, 7-13r

take

take after, 6-5

take back, 6-12

take in, 5-12, 6-6

take off, 5-15, 6-16

take over, 5-1

take to, 7-17r

take up, 6-6, 6-8

talent, 2-14

talk

talk over, 6-5

tall

taper, 7-16r

tardy, 7-2p

target, 4-17

task, 4-25, 5-10

taste, 3-15

tattered, 7-11r

tavern, 7-13r

tax, 3-18

taxi, 1-11

tea

teach

team, 1-10

tear, 5-13

tear down, 6-9

tear up, 5-13

tears, 1-25

technical, 3-24

technique, 4-9

technology, 3-10

telegram, 3-5

telephone

telescope, 3-10

television, 1-9

tell

tell off, 6-16

teller, 4-22

temper, 4-21

temper, 7-2r, 7-15r

temperament, 7-4p

temperamental, 7-4p

temperate, 3-11

temperature, 2-15, 5-2

temporary, 5-20

ten

tendency, 4-14

tenement, 7-5p

tenet, 7-6r

tennis, 1-10

tense, 4-4

tent, 4-4

tenure, 5-5

term, 4-22

terms, 4-22, 6-14

terrible, 2-10

territory, 5-22

terse, 7-15r

test

testimony, 5-25

textile, 5-15

thank

the

theater, 2-23

their

them

theme, 6-2

themselves

then

then, 3-23

theory, 4-23

therefore

thermal, 6-19

thermometer, 3-19

these

thesis, 5-5

they

thick, 2-9

thief, 5-25

thin

thing

think

think about, 6-12

think over, 6-6

think through, 5-12

think up, 5-12

third

this

those

thoughtless, 6-9

thousand

thread, 4-10

threat, 5-10

three

thrifty, 7-10p

throat, 5-2

through, 3-7

throw

throw away, 6-3

throw up, 6-17

thunder, 3-11

thus, 3-18

thwart, 7-14p

ticket, 1-2, 6-22

tide, 7-21p

tie, 1-17, 4-11, 5-20

tie up, 5-9

tight, 2-9

tile, 7-18p

tilt, 7-5r

time

tiny, 4-6

tip, 4-24

tire, 4-21

title, 2-17

toast, 4-16

toaster, 4-16

today

toddler, 7-4p

together, 2-20

tolerate, 6-4

tomorrow

tongue, 4-16

tonight

too

tool, 2-20

tooth

tooth, 2-6

top

topic, 2-17

torpedo, 7-16p

torture, 7-1p

total, 2-12

totalitarian, 7-20p

touch, 3-15

touch on, 5-4

tourist, 1-21

tournament, 5-20

toward, 3-8, 4-4

tower, 7-18p

town, 2-3

toxic, 6-17

trace, 6-12

tractor, 5-7

trade, 4-12

tradition, 4-10

traffic, 1-2

tragedy, 5-13

trail, 5-16

train

train, 2-20

trait, 6-24

transact, 6-14

transaction, 7-10r

transform, 6-22

transition, 5-8

translate, 2-17

transparent, 5-6

transplant, 6-17

transportation, 1-2

trap, 4-15

trash, 5-18

trauma, 7-22p

travel, 1-7

treachery, 7-7r

treason, 7-7p

treasure, 4-22

treat, 5-2

tree

tremendous, 6-9

trench, 7-8r

trend, 6-14

trespass, 7-16r

trial, 5-10

triangle, 4-13

tribe, 4-4

trick, 1-25

trigger, 7-12r

trip, 1-2, 6-22

troop, 5-9

troops, 5-9

tropical, 2-15

trouble, 1-20

truant, 7-6p

truce, 7-3p

truck, 3-3

true

trunk, 5-16

trust, 1-20

try

try on, 5-15

try out, 5-12

tube, 5-23

tuition, 1-8

turn, 1-11

turn down, 5-4

turn in, 6-8

turn into, 5-3

turn off, 6-9

turn on, 6-8

turn out, 6-9, 6-18

turn up, 5-12

turnout, 6-18

twelve

twenty

twice

twins, 2-5

twist, 3-19

two

type

typewriter, 2-1

typical, 2-15

tyrant, 7-7p

ugly, 1-17

ultimate, 4-14

umbrella

uncle

unconventional, 6-21

under, 2-15

undergo, 5-14

undergraduate, 2-19

underlying, 7-2p

understand

undertake, 6-4

undoubtedly, 3-18

uneasy, 5-3
unemployed, 2-20
unexpected, 3-24
unfit for, 4-9
unflagging, 7-2r
unfortunately, 1-14
unfurnished, 1-3
uniform, 3-20
union, 3-24
unique, 5-16, 6-19
unit, 5-3
unite, 5-22, 6-4
universal, 6-19
university
unless, 3-25
unlikely, 4-8
(un)lock, 2-7
unruly, 7-6p
untoward, 7-2r
up
upkeep, 7-18r
upset, 4-22
urban, 4-24
urgent, 6-11
us
use
use up, 6-3
useful, 1-19
usually/unusual, 1-4
utilities, 1-12
utility, 5-15
utopia, 6-16
utter, 7-12r

vacant, 3-16
vacation, 1-7
vague, 5-4
valid, 5-24
valley, 1-19
valuable, 2-7

vanish, 7-22r
vanquish, 7-16r
vapor, 5-3
various (vary), 2-23
vary, 5-12
vast, 5-3
vegetable, 1-19
vegetation, 5-3
vehement, 7-12p
vehicle, 3-3
velocity, 5-19
vengeance, 7-1r
ventilation, 7-5p
venture, 6-14
veranda, 7-5r
verdict, 5-25
versatile, 5-13
version, 5-4
vertigo, 7-9r
very
vessel, 6-11
vestibule, 7-18r
veteran, 6-20
veterinarian, 5-7
vex, 7-14r
via, 3-3
vibrate, 6-22
vice, 6-12
victim, 2-7
victory, 5-9
view, 3-8, 3-18
vigorous, 5-20
village, 3-17
violate, 5-19
visa, 5-1
visible, 5-18
vision, 5-23
visit, 1-7
vital, 6-9
vitamin, 6-3

vivid, 5-16
vocation, 6-2
voice, 1-24
volleyball, 4-21
volume, 3-6
voluntary, 3-20
vomit, 5-23
vote, 2-11
vouch for, 7-10p
voucher, 7-10p
vulnerable, 6-19

wage, 2-20
wail, 7-4r
waist, 5-15
wait
wait on, 6-11
wait up, 6-5
waiter, 4-25
wake
walk
walk back, 5-16
wall
wallet, 1-22
want
war, 1-18
ward, 7-4p
ward off, 7-22r
warm
warm, 3-24
warranty, 6-23
wary, 7-16r
wash
wash off, 5-3
wash out, 6-9
washout, 6-9
waste, 4-16
watch
water
wave, 1-23, 4-21, 6-11

way
way, 2-24
we
weak, 1-10
wealth, 5-10
weapon, 3-20
wear, 1-17
wear off, 5-15
wear out, 4-10, 5-15
weary, 7-22r
weather
weave, 5-15
wedding, 2-5
week
weigh/weight, 1-13
welcome, 3-16
welfare, 6-18
well
west
wet, 3-11
what
wheat, 1-19
wheel, 1-11
when
whenever, 3-8
where
which
whimper, 7-4r
whisper, 3-23
whistle, 5-19
white
white-collar, 4-25
who
whole, 4-21

whom
why
wide, 2-9
widespread, 6-17
widow, 4-18
widower, 4-18
wife
wild, 3-17
will
willing, 4-14
win, 1-10
wind, 1-4, 5-15
window, 1-6
wing, 4-19
winter
wipe, 6-13
wipe off, 6-22
wipe out, 6-20
wire, 4-11
wise, 3-25
wish, 2-11
with
withdrawal, 3-13
within, 3-6
without, 1-17
withstand, 6-21
witness, 5-10
woman (women)
wonder, 6-8
woo, 7-17r
wood, 2-3, 5-3
wool, 1-17
word
work

work out, 5-7, 5-12
world, 2-16
worry, 1-8
worship, 4-20
worth, 3-25
would
wound, 5-2
wrap, 3-5
wrath, 7-14r
wrinkle, 6-17
write
write down, 6-18
write out, 6-8
write up, 5-4
wrong

X-ray, 2-6

year
yell, 7-1r
yellow
yes
yesterday
yield, 5-7
you
young
your
yourself
yourselves
youth, 4-1

zero, 3-10
zipper, 7-11p
zone, 3-11
zoo, 2-18

Words in Volume 8

This index includes two units on the companion Web site.
Numbers refer to volume and unit.